CHANGE IS ON THE AIR

CHANGE IS ON THE AIR

How WZAK Became #1 in Cleveland

Lee Zapis

CLEVELAND, OH

First Parafine Press Edition 2019
ISBN: 978-1-950843-00-8

P
PARAFINE
PRESS
P

Parafine Press
3143 West 33rd Street, Cleveland, Ohio 44109
www.parafinepress.com

Cover design by David Wilson
Book design by Meredith Pangrace

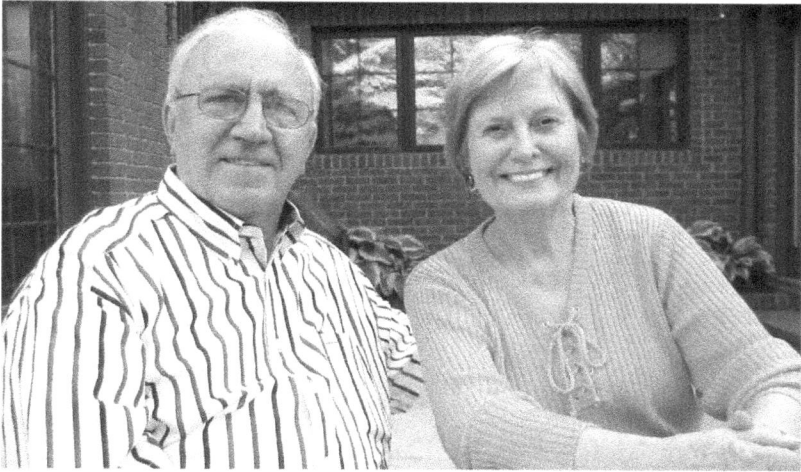

DEDICATION

I'd like to dedicate this book to the memory of my parents, Xen and Lula Zapis. When my father started his Greek radio program in 1949 followed by my mom joining him on the air in 1952 they never imagined that from those humble roots the urban WZAK would take hold. They showed me, through their example, what it takes to be successful: hard work; dedication; and putting your employees, listeners, and advertisers first.

I also want to thank my smart and beautiful wife Ageleke for her support over all these years. And for her encouragement to pursue projects that I felt excited about.

And I want to acknowledge my sisters, Maria, Donna and Renee for everything they did to make WZAK a success.

CONTENTS

INTRODUCTION

The early 1980s brought a lot of changes to the American culture. In 1981, MTV launched, IBM introduced the personal computer, and a year later the compact disc came along. 1981 was also the year that my tiny, family-owned radio station in Cleveland called WZAK changed formats to urban contemporary.

When we started programming urban contemporary music on WZAK, we had formerly featured nationality programs by various ethnic groups that were heavily represented in Cleveland—primarily Eastern European. We decided to shift focus and break into a market that was unfamiliar to us but seemed poised for growth. By the time we sold the station in 1999, as part of the most significant broadcast radio deal in local radio history, we were the number one radio station in Cleveland. We had racked up dozens of Billboard Radio Awards and, most significantly, had the highest power ratio (a measure of how well ratings are converted to revenue) of any urban contemporary station in the United States for years. Many songs that WZAK first played went on to become best selling singles; our radio airplay was responsible for launching the careers of numerous artists, including Mary J. Blige, Usher, Gerald Levert, MC Hammer, and more.

How did we become so successful? To a certain extent, we just happened to be in the right place at the right time. But we were also doing the right things. It just happened, and it was wildly successful. Yet our success also stemmed from a few key factors: the culture of the station we created, which flowed down from my father, Xenophon "Xen" Zapis; our respect for the black consumer; and the excellent team that we were able to assemble, including Mike Hilber as our General Sales Manager and Lynn Tolliver as our Program Director, who steered us through a difficult transition and made our little station a huge hit.

The success of WZAK was made up of three pillars: programming, sales, and promotions. Like a three-legged stool or the base of pyramid, these three pillars created a stable foundation for the ongoing success of WZAK. I believe that this solid foundation has served WZAK well over the years—and continues to. Almost forty years later, WZAK is still at or near the top of the ratings in Cleveland serving the listeners who grew up with the station and their kids.

What follows is the story of WZAK from my perspective and the lessons I learned that perhaps could help other business owners step outside their comfort zone and embrace change.

U.S. News & World Report Magazine Photograph Collection (Library of Congress)

THE ROOTS OF WZAK

My father, Xenophon "Xen" Zapis, was entrepreneurial minded from an early age. He was born in Cleveland on Bolivar Road, which was a Greek and Syrian enclave at the time. His father owned a coffee shop, and Xen lived with his parents and his older brother Danny lived in the apartments upstairs. For what my father knew of life, it was a happy time, surrounded by fellow Greek immigrants. But it wasn't a cushy childhood, either.

When he was a kid, my father was always looking for ways to earn extra money. He liked trying to come up with new business ideas. One of the many stories he told us about his various endeavors was how he would collect and resell tickets for the streetcar. The streetcar would run seven days a week, ferrying people from downtown to their neighborhoods. Most businessmen would buy weekly passes, good from Monday through Sunday. So my father would go hang out at the stop near his house on Friday afternoons. There, he would ask the exiting businessmen to give him their passes. There were still two days left on the passes, but

since most of them were not going to use the streetcar on the weekend, many happily gave them up. Then, my father would go back on Saturday evening and sell those passes to guys who were going out on dates, asking half of what they were going to pay for a regular one-day pass.

My father was always thinking of moneymaking ideas, and it was from those experiences that he developed his business savvy. My sisters and I absorbed all of those business lessons.

Another classic story from my dad's childhood was the importance of knowing your market. When his family moved out to another ethnic neighborhood near 79th and Woodland Avenue, he and one of his buddies decided to sell Christmas cards door-to-door. His godmother lived in nearby Cleveland Heights, which was a much wealthier part of town, and my father figured he could sell a lot of Christmas cards up there. So he and his friend took the streetcar to Cleveland Heights and spent the day going door-to-door trying to sell their cards. By the end of the day, they had only sold a box or two. He couldn't figure out why these wealthy people were so cheap, refusing to buy his perfectly nice cards, and for years he harbored a kind of resentment towards Cleveland Heights. Years later, after he was married to my mother, they were driving through Cleveland Heights, and he told her this story.

"But, dear, this is a Jewish neighborhood," she responded.

"What does that have to do with anything?" he said. And then the light bulb went off: Why would his Jewish neighbors want to buy Christmas cards? The lesson from that experience was to know your market. That was a key component to WZAK's future success as an urban radio station.

When my dad was only fourteen years old, his father passed away. My grandmother didn't read or write English, but she worked to support her two sons in the aftermath of the

In
One Third of
The FM - Homes
At Least ONE
Foreign Language
Is
Spoken

Great Depression and the loss of her husband. Meanwhile, my father attended John Hay High School in Cleveland and learned a lot of valuable business skills there. Later on, he pushed his own kids to learn these same business skills that would help us in the future. Today some would call it developing a "talent stack."

After being discharged from the Army, my father moved back to Cleveland. He had a dream, after the war, of moving to California, because it seemed so full of opportunities. California in the late forties must have seemed like a paradise compared to Cleveland. However, his loyalty and obligation to his mother kept him in Cleveland.

My dad met my mother, Smaragda "Lula" Petrakis, here in Cleveland. She came to Cleveland after the end of World War II and the Greek Civil War that followed. My parents both graduated from John Hay High School, but they met at the Annunciation Greek Orthodox Church in Tremont.

My father graduated from Fenn College, and then got his law degree at John Marshall Law School. He practiced law for a number of years, and for a short time, he co-owned an appliance store at 72nd and St. Clair that sold and repaired TVs and other appliances. He did a lot of real estate investing and developing and owned a number of rental properties.

In 1949, my father had the idea of producing and hosting a radio program for the Greek community of Greater Cleveland. He had heard different nationality radio shows on various stations around town and thought there should be a radio program for the Greek community. So he walked into a local station, (I think it was WSRS) introduced himself to the general manager and said, "I'd like to have a Greek program."

"Yeah, sure," the guy said. "We're happy to give you an hour program. It's fifty bucks an hour."

"How am I going to afford that?" my father asked.

"You have to go out and sell ads," the man responded.

So my dad went out and got about twelve local businesses to pay five dollars each for an ad. The advertisers were all small businesses: funeral homes, Greek-owned diners, grocery stores, etc. He paid fifty dollars to the station, and made a profit of ten dollars. My father produced the show, played records, and read news from Greece, and made ten bucks a week.

After my parents married in 1952, my mother became the co-host of the radio show and, in my opinion, the star. She would read the news in Greek, and then my dad would do the same in English. They also produced events, such as "The First All-Greek Stage Show and Dance," which my father emceed just two weeks after I was born. It was held at the Towne Club on Prospect Avenue and included gymnasts, a violinist, a classical soprano, pianists, Greek comedy, and "exotic Syrian dancing." The advertisers included John Costa, a furrier who had shops on Carnegie and Huron; Jean's Museum and Penny Arcade on East 9th Street; Olympia Confectionary at 55th and Broadway; Samos Wholesale Grocery on Bolivar Road; and the Eleniss Sheet Metal Company on Madison—just to name a few. The same formula, a station-sponsored event, would become a cornerstone of the future WZAK and eventually the radio biz overall.

At first, the radio show was just a hobby, but it slowly became a more significant part of their lives. And because of the program, everybody in the Northeast Ohio Greek

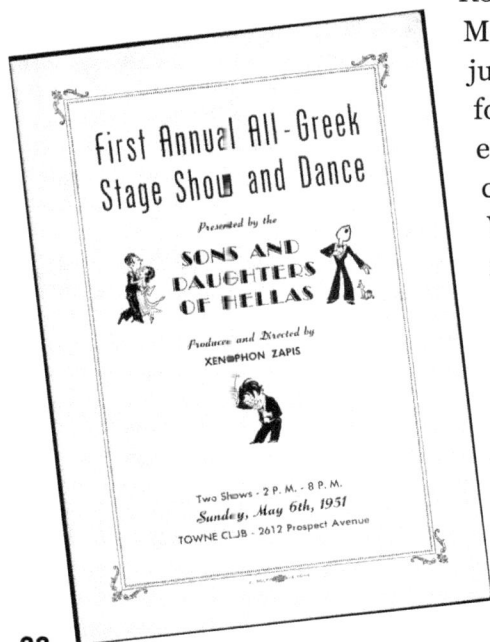

First Annual All-Greek
Stage Show and Dance

Presented by the

SONS AND
DAUGHTERS
OF HELLAS

Produced and Directed by
XENOPHON ZAPIS

Two Shows - 2 P. M. - 8 P. M.
Sunday, May 6th, 1951
TOWNE CLUB - 2612 Prospect Avenue

community knew my parents. Whenever somebody died, got engaged or married, or had relatives come over from Greece for a visit, people would call my father up to let them know, and my parents would announce it on the radio. They were celebrities of sorts because the community all listened to the show. People would recognize them on the street. Early on, he was nicknamed "the little Greek Walter Winchell," after a well-known news personality of the time.

My parents produced their Greek radio program on a number of radio stations in Cleveland including WXEN. Many people thought that they owned that station because the call letters were my dad's first name. I was told that the station got those call letters because each ethnic producer at the time submitted their idea for new call letters and WXEN was the one available.

In early 1962, the Ohio Muzak Corporation approached my father and some other ethnic radio producers from WXEN to invest in a new FM radio station. The Ohio Muzak Corporation did not want to run a radio station; they wanted to have access to an FM signal to distribute their programming. At that time, everyone who subscribed to Muzak had specialized radios, which received the programming via a part of the FM signal called a subcarrier. Muzak was a service that offered background music to office and other locations. It was also known as "elevator music". My father and only three other producers decided to join forces. The other two were producers of German radio programs: Joe and Betty Bauer, who had immigrated to the US after WWII, and Bob Stumpf, who owned a business called Kitchen Made Meats at the West Side Market and did their radio show as a hobby. The three of them each put up $7,500, and the Ohio Muzak Corporation contributed the construction permit and the eventual license to build WZAK. The ZAK in the call letters came from Muzak.

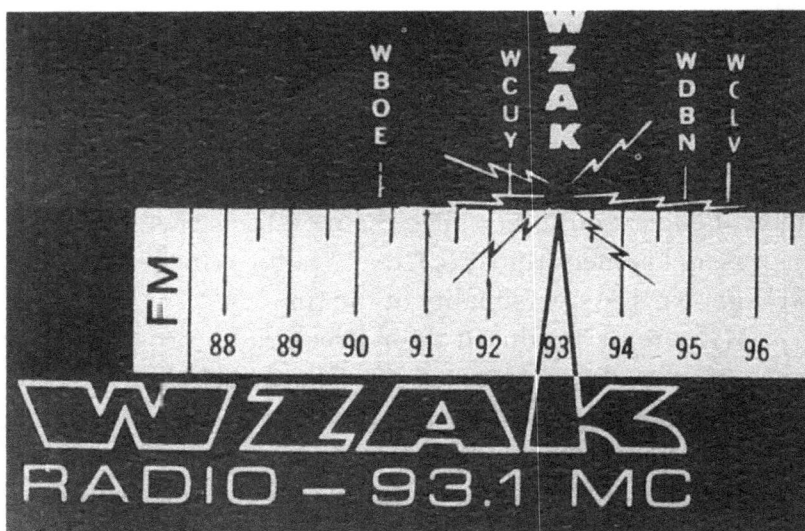

WZAK RADIO – 93.1 MC

In high school, my sister Maria and I started working at the station during the summers, cleaning up the record library, filing, and performing other tasks. Slowly, we got more involved with the operation of the station. Back in those days, even the on-air DJ had to take a test to get a third-class FCC license in order to "operate" a radio station transmitter. When I was sixteen, my dad drove me to Detroit to take the certification test at the FCC field office. I was pretty proud of myself when I passed. After I graduated high school, I went to Cleveland State, volunteered at WCBS, the college radio station, and received a bachelor's degree in communications. I worked at WZAK part-time during my college years. The offices were a few blocks away from the CSU campus, so I'd go over and work on occasion. One summer I was the board operator from 10:00 p.m. on Saturday night to 8:00 a.m. on Sunday morning. Back then, Prospect and 13th was a pretty dicey neighborhood. I'd drive down to the station and hope to find a parking space in front of the building, wishing there wasn't a hooker hanging out in the vestibule. I'd run to the door and try to unlock it as fast as possible then get in and lock it behind me before someone came along. The guy I was relieving would put on a tape, and then I'd head downstairs and let him out and lock the door. Then I'd walk up four flights of steps because the elevator was old, and you wouldn't want to risk getting stuck between floors when you were the only person in the building. I'd walk into that small little studio and run prerecorded public affairs tapes, taking meter readings and try to stay awake. I dozed off more times than I can remember, but I never missed a show.

On Sunday morning, I'd have to make sure the Polish program with A.W. Zebrowski got on the air. I remember one time specifically when 7:00 a.m. came along, I pushed the wrong button on the console and broadcast nothing but dead air. Moments later the hotline lit up in the studio. A very Mr. Zebrowski was calling to express his displeasure. I can't recall everything he said but he was not pleased with the inept board operator on duty that morning. Not one of my better moments.

One-third of the FM-listening homes in the area spoke at least one foreign language at home. There were Greeks, Italians, and Slovaks, all relocating here to Cleveland. Cleveland was full of Eastern Europeans coming over to work in the steel mills. It was a land of opportunity. There were lots of refugees from the war, and a lot of highly educated Hungarians arrived after the revolution in 1956. The famous Hollywood screenwriter Joe Eszterhas was a young Hungarian kid who worked at WZAK for a few years. I met him a few years ago at a speech and book signing. I introduced myself, and he was kind enough to write an inscription to my dad in his book, saying "To my favorite boss."

In 1967, WZAK also sold time to Barry Weingart and Steve "Doc Nemo" Nemeth for a show that featured progressive rock. It aired late Saturday nights. I used to wonder what the history of the station would have been if my parents and Joe & Betty Bauer had recognized the changing landscape of FM sooner. The station also had some brokers who featured jazz and oldies over the years.

By 1971, we were airing programs in fourteen different languages: Croatian, Czech, German, Greek, Hindi, Hungarian, Italian, Polish, Serbian, Slovak, Slovenian, Spanish—and a British show. A.W. Zebrowski, the producer of our Polish show, programmed almost forty hours of Polish shows every week out of his studio in Richfield, Ohio. We ran ads in all those languages in the *Cleveland Press* to promote the shows beyond the ethnic communities. In 1974, we hosted an ethnic festival to "present a more accurate image of the ethnics, different from the conventional entertainment, by combining a folklore show with dancing and an exhibition of imported goods, as well as ethnic antiques."

The advertisers in those days were still little mom-and-pop grocery stores, butcher shops, candy stores, and travel agencies. We had funeral homes and wedding halls, too. A lot of them were on Fleet Avenue, which was a big Polish area. On East 185th, around Waterloo, there was a significant Slovenian neighborhood with businesses that often advertised on the Slovenian shows. Businesses on Lorain Avenue near the West Side Market advertised on the German shows.

With so many languages we had to have people in the community who would listen to the station and report back to make sure no one was saying anything subversive or inappropriate. Sometimes the shows caused tension. For example, John Birek, a nice guy who lived near 36th and St. Clair, did our Croatian show. One night, during the movement to break up Yugoslavia, a Croatian separatist bombed his house because he wasn't nationalist enough. Croatians wanted to have their own, independent nation,

ΕΝΔΙΑΦΕΡΟΝΤΑ ΝΕΑ ΚΑΘΕ ΒΡΑΔΥ ΣΤΑΣ 7:00 M. M.
GREEK NEWS NIGHTLY AT 7:00 P. M.

CHURCH NEWS

COMMUNITY NEWS

ENGAGEMENTS

WEDDINGS

BIRTHS

CHRISTENINGS

ANNIVERSARIES

DEDICATIONS

CLUB NEWS

•

Only $3.00

Call MA 1-7897

•

LISTEN TO THE PLEASANT CONTINENTAL SOUND
on
WZAK-FM
93.1MC

WZAK - fm 93.1

FUNERALS

MNIMOSINA

GRADUATIONS

BON VOYAGE

DANCES

PICNICS

BUSINESS OPENINGS

GET WELL WISHES

ETC., ETC.

•

Only $3.00

Call 333-3680

•

XENOPHON ZAPIS, President of WZAK

THE GREEK RADIO PROGRAM
WZAK - FM   93.1 m. c.
STUDIOS AND OFFICES IN DOWNTOWN CLEVELAND — 1303 PROSPECT AVENUE

The Greek Radio Programs are sponsored by these Loyal, Civic-Minded Merchants

SAMOS GROCERY CO.
S. S. QUEEN FREDERIKA
CHEF LOUIS RESTAURANT
RUSYNYK-YURCH Funeral Homes
TOWER INSURANCE AGENCY
ATHENIAN RESTAURANT
LAUB BAKING CO.
ANGELO DAMALAS' SWAMP
SCOCOS PLUMBING CO.
SHAKER LEE HALL

CRYSTAL DISTRIBUTING CO.
STREMANOS-JANIS Monument Co.
CLEVELAND REFRIGERATION CO.
G. & N. MEAT CO., Akron
PAPPAS REALTY CO., Akron
JOHN PETROU INSURANCE, Akron
BROWN DERBY Restaurants, Akron
BOSWELL JONES Funeral Home
J. DeNUNZIO IMPORTED FOODS

GRECIAN GARDENS
PARMA SAVINGS CO.
UNIVERSE MOTORS
GALLUCCI GROCERY CO.
COOLEY DODGE CARS
W. & W. MEAT CO.
EUROPA TRAVEL SERVICE
STAN'S, STUDIO
DORIC ROOM

BRIDGE HOME BAKERY
TAVERNA GRAPEVINE
SMERDAS FURNITURE CO.
TOP REALTY CO.
JAN JEWELERS
LOIKA LAMB MARKET
ALESCI'S Imported Foods
BLAZEK SEA FOODS
G. & D. BUILDERS

Please Patronize Our Advertisers — They Bring You The Greek Program

but all John wanted to do was play music.

By the late seventies, Bob Stumpf, one of the original investors in WZAK approached my father and asked him if he'd be interested in buying his shares of the company. Mr. Stumpf was more focused on his meat company and thought it was good time to sell his shares. My father immediately said yes and signed a purchase agreement that week. A couple of years later my parent's other partners, Joe and Betty Bauer, eventually decided to retire and agreed to sell their shares to my parents. They eventually bought out the Ohio Muzak Corporation, making them the sole owner of WZAK.

As Bob Dylan said "the times were a changing." On March 21, 1977, WXEN switched their format to Top 40 and changed the call letters to WZZP. The station moniker became ZIP 106. At that time the FCC could get involved in format decisions, and if they felt your station provided a unique voice in the community they could block a format change. After WXEN switched away from ethnic programming we were concerned that we might not be able to change formats ourselves, because we were the only full-time FM ethnic station remaining in the community. A court case in 1981 decided the FCC could no longer impose such restrictions.

In 1977, the *Cleveland Press* ran a story called the "Passing of Ethnic Radio." Joe Bauer, then the general manager and part owner of WZAK, was quoted as saying "The Big Business establishment, in its arrogance, disregards and ignores ethnic broadcasting which is replacing foreign-language newspapers. They won't advertise on our stations, but they give lip service: 'How cute the dancers look in their colorful costumes. How neat and well-maintained these people keep their property!'"

We could see the writing on the wall. Five years later, we would abandon the ethnic format and rebrand as an urban contemporary station, serving Cleveland's black community. To succeed in our new format, we would have to build the three pillars of our foundation—programming, sales, and promotion—from the ground up.

Sometimes you don't to be a WINNER.

Lyn

93 FM WZAK

have to be on top

Tolliver Jr.

THE PROGRAMMING PILLAR

By becoming a majority owner of WZAK, my father was able to create a format that he had been thinking about for a number of years. The idea was to play a mix of music that would broadly appeal to the various nationality groups—Poles, Slovenians, Greeks, Hungarians, Germans, etc. It would be easy listening, like Muzak but with an international flair.

My father hired Wayne Mack, who was a legendary radio personality in Cleveland and who worked at WDOK, to program the station and be its primary host. The experiment lasted less than a year. In that first year, we played the international instrumental music mix from 6:00 a.m. to 6:00 p.m. Then, from 6:00 p.m. to sign off and on weekends we aired the traditional ethnic programming.

The new weekday format was overly broad and although it had something for everyone, it didn't have enough for any specific audience. Also, by 1980 some of the ethnic producers were retiring or passing away. So even during the evening and weekend ethnic programming hours, we had fewer producers, fewer people interested in becoming producers, and fewer listeners. That formula meant declining revenues. My sister Maria and I thought the station had potential, but not if we continued with this new format. We were more of a public service station than a commercial radio station.

While we were programming this easy listening/ beautiful music format we were approached by Cleveland radio air personality Larry Morrow. He wanted to buy the station. He mounted a quite the charm offensive, but we knew we were sitting on a potential gold mine and weren't interested in selling. My sister and I—only twenty-four and twenty-three respectively—had only limited experience in the radio business. But we had a hunch we could do more with our station if we changed the format.

We started exploring other format opportunities. We received a lot of support from Gordon Stenbach, who was the general manager of WZZP. He encouraged us to look into other formats that might make sense for the region. TM Century, the program syndicator, did a very rudimentary market survey to see where the format holes were in Cleveland radio. They

93FM

WZAK 1303 PROSPECT AVENUE CLEVELAND, OHIO 44115

LEE ZAPIS
Operations Manager

(216)621-9300

added up the share that rock stations, easy listening stations, country stations, and others had, and then divided that number by the number of stations airing each format. We saw that urban contemporary had a very high share of the market (12) but there were only two-and-a-half stations (WDMT-FM, WJMO-AM, and one AM daytimer, WABQ) playing music for the black consumer. So to our way of thinking, there was a hole in the market for urban contemporary.

Urban contemporary was a term coined in the early eighties. It was a blend of contemporary R&B, smooth jazz, and some crossover pop music. It was meant to appeal to an African American audience between the ages of eighteen and forty-four. The black community didn't have a lot of choices back then. Adult blacks were listening to the same stuff that young blacks were listening to. These days there's a much bigger delineation in music in the black community today than there was at that time. Now you have black adult contemporary (older music for older blacks), hip-hop and rap. Early on, I thought that rap music was a passing fad and that as soon as white kids started rapping the black community would move away from it. But rap and hip-hop just became more and more popular.

Our market survey was very amateurish, but that was how we made our decision to shift formats. If you were going to do something like this today, you'd probably undertake a $50,000 study to look at the holes in the marketplace, vulnerabilities of other stations, etc. But armed only with the data from that one half-baked survey and a strong feeling in our gut, we decided WZAK would become an urban contemporary station.

Now we had to figure out how to become an urban contemporary station. We settled on using the programming syndicator TM Century to help us program the station. Located in Dallas, TM Century would send us preprogrammed music tapes every week. It was buying a format in a box. That was what we started using when we changed the format in March 1981.

Our first hire for the new format was Harry Osibin—or Harry "O," as he called himself. Harry O came from St. Louis and knew Jack Patterson, the creator of the TM Century urban contemporary format. Patterson recommended Harry O to us because they had worked together in the past. Harry showed up at the station on his first day and brought his dog, DJ, with him. DJ promptly urinated on a column in the lobby. Harry became our PD and afternoon air talent.

Changing formats was logistically tricky and controversial, as WXEN had shown. It was also painful to dismiss the ethnic producers. My parents had worked with them for many years and had personal relationships with most of them. Their contract stated we had to give them thirty days notice before ending their shows, but we were worried about giving them that much notice because when WXEN did the same thing a few years earlier the producers used their radio shows to rally their listeners to protest. They even got politicians involved to try to stop the switch. We were not going to let that happen to us. So we decided to allow some of them to continue airing their shows on Sundays only. My father's attorney, Thano Pasalis, met with the most successful producers and told them: "Here's the story. You don't get a chance to say goodbye to your listeners, but you can still be on air on Sundays." That helped mute the response of the programmers.

The Polka Convoy was the last ethnic radio show to air on the old format. The next day, at 6:00 a.m. on March 2, 1981, Rich Kenney kicked off the new WZAK with a song called "Fancy Dancer" by the disco/jazz fusion band Twennynine. WZAK was now an urban contemporary radio station.

I can't describe the excitement we all felt. Even now when I listen to that first song we played, the memories come flooding back. That morning our phone lines were overloaded. "Something's wrong with my radio," they said. "I can't hear the right music." I felt awful. We all did. When we went to church the following Sunday, everyone told us how much they missed the Greek show, which for many had been their only connection to their homeland. It was heartbreaking. I could relate to them, as a child of immigrants myself. And I understood that the end of the radio programs was a sign of other changes happening in their own lives. The connection to the old country was eroding further.

The response in the local news media was mixed. *The Plain Dealer* ran an article on March 9, 1981, that said, of the shift in format, "traditionally isolated ethnic groups are being assimilated into the mainstream of American life. The real dividend is that Cleveland may, as a result, be shedding its Achilles' heel: Crippling contentiousness among the nationality groups."

There were also concerns about black radio. An op-ed in the same paper on April 12, 1981, asked: "Where is black radio?" It noted that of the four stations playing black music at the time—WABQ, WJMO, WDMT, and us—none were black-owned. "A major part of the black community's complaint is that the predominantly white-owned stations, as well as the white-owned businesses that advertise on them, are engaging in economic carpet bagging." Carl Stokes, the former mayor who had left Cleveland for New York and was doing radio broadcasting there, tried to start a black-owned station, but it never came to fruition. Ultimately, though, because we were committed to serving the black community and were locally owned, unlike the other stations, we never received much pushback.

At the time, radio had to follow the Federal Communications Act of 1934, which stated that radio broadcasters had to serve the public interest. That means that listeners could have challenged our license, saying that we were not serving the public by switching formats and losing the nationality programming.

Because of the pain the transition caused to our former listeners, but primarily to maintain some revenue during this period of abrupt change, we kept airing those ethnic programs on Sunday. Our schedule in 1981 was Polish programming from 6:00–9:00 a.m., German from 9:00–10:30 a.m., Croatian from 10:30 a.m.–12:00 p.m., Slovenian from 12:00–4:00 p.m., Spanish from 4:00–6:00 p.m., Greek from 6:00–7:00 p.m. Italian from 7:00–9:00 p.m., and Hungarian from 9:00–10:00 p.m. We dropped the Arabic, French, British, Irish, Indian, Slovak, and Serbian programs, along with the Polka Convoy. But after about a year of this schizophrenic programming, I convinced my dad that we had to be urban contemporary 24/7. We spent all week trying to grow our new audience, then spent Sundays driving them away.

Since we were playing preprogrammed shows we purchased from the syndicator at the beginning, there wasn't a lot of interaction between DJs and the audience. The music was delivered to us each week on three reel-to-reel tapes that we would play in sequence: the first tape contained the Top 10 hits, the second was upcoming hits, and the third played oldies. The DJs did not have any flexibility when it came to choosing what music to play or how much they could say between songs. Nevertheless, after we changed the format, we had a solid showing in the first Arbitron report, a quarterly ratings analysis of listener share. Most of that was due to people having something new to listen to and a lower spot load. It wasn't because we were well-programmed.

These preprogrammed shows would have been adequate in a noncompetitive market, but we had three other radio stations competing for the African-American listener. Our main competitors were WDMT 107.9FM, which had evolved from a disco format, and WJMO 1490AM, a well-known and long-serving AM station for the black community. Since they were on the AM dial, WJMO had a limited signal and less fidelity than FM stations, and it was high up in the dial at 1490. WABQ 1540AM was the other competing station, but they could only broadcast from sunrise to sunset because of some arcane FCC rule. We tried to stand out from our competition by offering more music, which wasn't hard to do because we had so few commercials! We played about 85 percent black artists at the time. White musicians who sometimes ventured into R&B like the Doobie Brothers and Elton John were included on the tapes we got from TM Century. We played more music than the other stations and tried to let the personalities of the DJs shine. We wanted the audience to identify with the announcers. And we worked to build a bond with the community.

We plugged away, trying to figure out how to manage the transition, and learning what we needed to do better. One of my father's greatest strengths was that he knew what he didn't know. We knew we had to find people who were experts in the areas where we were weak. Luckily, we had great advisors (primarily Gordon Stenback) who were honest and straight with us about those weaknesses, and so we set out to make new hires to fill in those gaps.

Even though we were making progress we felt that we needed to up our game when it came to our programming. When we first went on the air with the urban format from TM Productions called "Alpha I." It was first developed by Jack Patterson the former PD at Houston's KMJQ. About three weeks after we signed our agreement with TM, Patterson took a job as program director of WBMX/Chicago with his former boss, Jim Maddox, who was the GM there. Patterson continued to program the TM Alpha I format for us but after approximately two months at WBMX, he left the TM group altogether. We were left to fend for ourselves which in hindsight was probably the best thing to happen to us in those early days.

It was a real mess; TM didn't help us with our growing pains at all. I think TM is a fine organization for programming in secondary markets, but I don't think that they were used to having their formats compete in major markets. They just really turned out to be a tape service. Looking back on things, their original consultation with us was pretty unrealistic. They said that after three months we should be well on our way to being sold out.

We knew Lynn Tolliver because as the regional rep for MCA Records urban division, he used to come by each week to bring us new music to play. Whenever Lynn came to the station he always had a smile on his face. He had a spirit about him that made you want to be around him. And he also sported a major jheri curl! Lynn lived and breathed radio and records. When he was a kid he would call the local record stores to see which records were popular so he could create is how hit list.

Cleveland had its own music taste and local preferences but because we were using a syndicated music service, we didn't play songs anything that weren't approved by TM Century. Lynn had worked in radio since he was seventeen or eighteen years old starting at WJMO. For a while Lynn was doing a radio show in Columbus and working as a mailman in Cleveland. Each day he would deliver the mail, then drive to Columbus for his air shift. After his air shift, he would drive back to Cleveland and start the process all over! Some may call that lunacy. I call it dedication.

Ray Calabrese was managing a hot local band called the Dazz Band at the time. They were blowing up across the county with their big hit "Let It Whip." Ray was a regular visitor to the station. He became one of my favorite people and someone I still run into here in town. Ray will always hold a special place in the heart of the Zapis family. Ray encouraged us to consider hiring Lynn as our program director and on-air personality. The more we got to know Lynn, the more we liked him. I'll never forget a comment Lynn made to me a few years after he came to work with us. He said "there's was nothing new under the sun, just new combinations." I can't count how many times I've thought about that philosophy and how it informed a lot of the things we did at the radio station. Nothing we did was revolutionary, but the way we combined things made us stand out from the crowd. (Thanks Lynn for your wisdom!)

Being a record rep was just a job for Lynn, and it involved a lot of travel—which he did not like. Plus, he was living in Detroit at the time and wanted to return to Cleveland where his mom and his sister and her family lived. We offered Lynn less than what he was making at MCA (the music biz typically paid more than the radio biz), but being able to come back home and program a new station was enough motivation for him to accept.

When Lynn came aboard in the spring of 1982, we had a group of air personalities that he had not hired. Nevertheless, he was able to coach them and got them to buy into his philosophy. They improved their on-air performance, but the team was still not up to his standards. He slowly began to put his mark on the staff. He was able to attract talent drawn to his passion, enthusiasm, and the opportunity to create a new radio station. Over the years Tolliver assembled an incredible team of air personalities: Kym Sellers, Kim Johnson, Ralph Poole, Bobby Rush, Lankford Stephens, Mike Love, Jeffrey Charles, Kim "Lady Skill" Skillern, David Tolliver (his nephew), and Antonio "Banana" Marshall. This core of talent became immersed in the community, worked hard, and all bought into the premise that what was best for the station would ultimately benefit them in the long term. We had other jocks come and go, and some of them were very good—Ken Allen and Eric Faison are two that I thought were standouts—but that core was the foundation for everything we did on the air. Our on-air personalities were real pros.

ralph POOLE

"3'S COMPANY"
"JUST THE 2 OF US"

FAVORITE FOOD: HAMBURGER
& FENCH FRIES
FAVORITE COLOR: RED

kym SELLERS

"3'S COMPANY"

FAVORITE FOOD: PIZZA
FAVORITE COLOR: PURPLE

FAVORITE FOOD: CAJUN CATFISH
FAVORITE COLOR: BLUE

bobby RUSH

"FOR LOVERS ONLY"

One of my pet peeves was when DJs thought it was okay for them to do their air shift while their friends were in the studio with them, and we put a stop to that practice quickly. Did the guy at the Ford plant have his buddy watching him put wheels on the car? We wanted everyone to take the job seriously. Lankford Stevens—Lankford "The Man" Stevens—was the consummate professional. His studio was always immaculate; he would show up early with his briefcase, prep, and do his show.

A few months after Lynn joined us, The Time released a single called "777-9311." Talk about a gift! Lynn took the record into the production room and dubbed "FM" over the hook "777-9311" so what people heard was "777-93FM". We played the heck out of that song and every other urban/black station in town wouldn't play it. That's an example of the creativity that Lynn brought to the station.

The early 1980s were a great era for urban music. Prince released his breakthrough album "1999" in October 1982. And just one month later we were delivered another thrilling gift, Michael Jackson's *Thriller* album. We played virtually every track from *Thriller* for the next year. It went on to become the biggest selling album of all time and WZAK. Another influential song from the early eighties was "I Need A Freak" by Sexual Harassment, a studio group put together by our own Lynn Tolliver. The song was released in 1983 but had a long life on the charts and because a huge hit. It has been samples and recorded a number of times most famously by the Black Eyed Peas for their song "My Humps."

A turning point in our development was when we started reporting our playlist to *Radio & Records* in 1983. That was a big deal. It legitimized the station to the industry. At the time our slogan was "WZAK, The Rhythm of the City."

Using the latest technology to give us an edge always appealed to me. We were the first station in Cleveland to

play songs directly from CDs. The sound quality was better, but it had more to do with audience perception. Before every song that we played from a CD, we played an imaging spot alerting the audience that they were listening to a CD. I doubt anyone could hear the difference, but we sounded cutting edge. That was important in the black community.

We were also the first station in town that started using a digital audio playback system in their main studio. This was back when a 10 MB hard drive cost $1,000! But we made the plunge and bought a system from a company called Arrakis and put all of our commercials into the digital audio workstations in the on-air studios. It made for easier use by the DJs and it was more efficient. I could see that the future was going to be digital. We might as well take the plunge and be ahead of the curve.

By 1984, we were being taken seriously in Cleveland. We were beating WDMT, up to that point the leading urban station in the market at the time. We had a 5.3 share of the market in the fall 1984 Arbitron report that put us in seventh place; WDMT had a 3.8 share and that landed them in eleventh place. That book made us the number one among black listeners. We spent $150,000 on giveaways and promotions to get our name out. We produced a marketing piece that we sent out to local and national advertisers that won an award from the National Radio Broadcasters Association. The title was "Black is Beautiful on the Bottom Line"—which convinced sponsors to advertise to our listeners. For many years the black consumer was ignored by a lot of mainstream advertisers. I'm convinced that it was more of a case of them not being pitched to properly and less a result of racism although I'm sure racism was a factor.

LAST HALF OF STORY MYSTERIOUSLY VANISHES !

Urban Warfare on Cleveland's Airwaves

93FM WZAK

1729 SUPERIOR AVENUE, SUITE 401,
CLEVELAND, OHIO 44114 (216) 621-9300

THE HOME OF "FOURPLAY"

Program director and announcer Lynn Tolliver Jr. with WZAK station owner Xenophon Zapis and his son, Lee Zapis, operations manager. Ratings have climbed since Tolliver came to the station in May 1982.

Check it out

The Four radio stations — WDMT, WZAK, WJMO and WABQ — directly aim at Cleveland's black audience, but only FM stations WDMT and WZAK hold ratings worthy of major advertisers' attention. Their battle for listeners has become a horse race; in the most recent Arbitron book, WZAK got 5.2% of all radio listeners measured and WDMT got 3.8, ranking them 7th and 11th, respectively. (These figures reflect Arbitron's polling of all listeners in the metropolitan area, 12 years old and up, from sign-on to sign-off of each week in the rating period.)

Of the other two, which once were the only stations aimed at blacks here, WJMO is a relatively low-rated AM music-and-variety station and WABQ is a daytime-only AM station featuring religious programs and gospel music. Church groups buy time, so WABQ doesn't seek advertising.

The growth of the urban-contemporary sound has resulted partly from the growth of FM radio and has, in turn, led to a renewed popularity of so-called black music.

Through the 1960s, Cleveland's airwaves were dominated by the Top-40 pop sound of AM stations like WIXY, WHK and WKYC, which included everything from Frank Sinatra tunes to the music of the Beatles and Barry Gordy's fledgling Motown.

But when the Federal Communications Commission decreed that broadcasters could not run the same signal on AM and FM sister stations — and automakers started putting FM receivers in cars — a demand for more sounds was created on FM. That helped to end the reign of the relatively broad-based Top-40, as each sub-

And we were the presenting radio station for one of the biggest R&B concerts ever held in Cleveland. The Plum Fest, held at Cleveland Municipal Stadium on August 13, 1984. More than 29,000 people came out to see Gladys Knight, Kashif, The Temptations, Aretha Franklin, and Maze. The Plum Fest was not only a commercial success but also a meaningful concert for R&B and soul artists nationally. You might ask why the event was called the Plum Fest. I'm not sure who came up with the name but it was to try to piggyback on a marketing campaign that the *Plain Dealer* came up with that said "If New York is the Big Apple, Cleveland's a Plum." Probably the lamest branding ever created to promote Cleveland.

We switched to the urban contemporary format right when rap was starting to break out. The first commercial rap record was Sugar Hill Gang's "Rapper's Delight," in 1979, so we were right on the cusp of rap breaking big time. And then you could see a cultural shift when black music became more popular during The Jacksons' Victory Tour in the summer and fall of 1984. We were so excited to hear they were going to tour and that Cleveland's own Don King Productions was producing, but WMMS who had recently switched from album oriented rock to contemporary hit radio decided to sponsor the tour in Cleveland. They had booked two nights, October 19 and 20 at the old Cleveland Lakefront Municipal Stadium. WMMS guaranteed a sellout: If the shows didn't sell out, they were going to be out hundreds of thousands of dollars, if not more. I'm not sure if they did end up selling it out or not. The concert business is a bit "fuzzy" so to speak. Nevertheless, we felt WMMS was encroaching on our turf. The Jacksons, and especially Michael Jackson, were our artist!

We needed to attach ourselves to this blockbuster of an event. We pulled out all the stops and secured tickets to give away on the air. We brought in Rebbie Jackson, Michael's

WZAK Grows Up

WALT LOVE

Cleveland Renegade Mellows, Tops Market

For the past ten years, **Zapis Communications' WZAK** has defended Cleveland's Urban crown from all comers. This summer, **Birch** showed the station — known for its renegade attitude — topping the general market arena for the first time on the strength of an 8.6-10.2 12+ increase. The **Arbitron** was also up on a 6.9-8.8 12+ jump.

In the mid-'80s, WZAK found itself in political hot water with Cleveland's black leadership and City Hall, thanks to what some called renegade programming decisions. Recently, ten-year PD/morning man **Lynn Tolliver** dismissed those frictions as bygones, saying, "We're growing up . . . like a kid who's been mischievous but has matured. We don't make the mistakes we made in the past. Now we not only want to win as we did in the past, but we know how to win with class."

Tolliver and Zapis Communications VP **Lee Zapis** addressed the station's current success and positioning. Tolliver credited some of the success to the fact that, "As PD, I've been very responsive to the black community. Recently, slower music has been a very strong variable in our daily music mix. I don't know why listeners want more ballads, but I do know they have more concrete messages. People can relate to ballads more than they can to any other form of music available right now.

"We've also been more consistent in programming our announcers. Instead of changing people's shifts after three to six months, we've left people in place so the public can get used to hearing the same voice and the same approach on the air.

"Because our announcers are truly personalities, we don't tie their hands when they're on the air — they can all perform and entertain. Since my morning co-host

Lee Zapis

Kim Johnson joined the show six months ago, she's sparked my own performance. She's been with the station for about five years, and used to do middays. Now **Matt Morton** does middays, **Langford Stevens** does afternoons from 3-8pm, and **Bobby Rush** does the love songs show from 8pm-1am. All our people do five-hour shifts."

Research Helps

Zapis noted, "We use the **Research Group** and approximately two or three times a year we commission research projects to help us determine what we should and shouldn't be doing. This way we stay on top of things before anything gets out of control with our programming approach. I think you have to project to the changes in your market as opposed to looking at the results of Arbitron and Birch numbers and then saying, 'Oh, we should have done this.'"

oldest sister, to come in for a series of station sponsored events. Rebbie had a hit record out at the time called "Centipede" which Michael had written and produced. Rebbie and her husband came in for the weekend of shows and we spend a lot of time together. She was a wonderful person and her husband Nate was equally as nice. Her appearance helped us be a part of the Jackson Victory tour. We stayed friends for a number of years and I was fortunate to be able to attend a handful of Michael Jackson's Bad Tour with Rebbie and her family. And it was through that relationship that I was able to meet Michael a few times. One of the highlights of my career.

Also shaking up the airwaves in 1984 was the release of Prince's single "I Would Die 4 U." But it wasn't the A-side of the single that caused the controversy. It was the B-side, "Erotic City." As usual, we were right in the middle of that controversy and playing a game of high risk, high reward.

By early October, "Erotic City," was being played by at numerous urban radio stations. At several of those stations "Erotic City" hit number one. Walt Love from *Radio & Records* covered the story from a national perspective and included us in his article because were one of the stations in a large market that was struggling with whether to play an edited version or go with the original. As Walt pointed out, "That song refueled the debate over playing songs with suggestive lyrics. One artist's phenomenal popularity, a hard-to edit track, and seventeen apparent uses of the word 'fuck' have put some programmers in a difficult position where they face complaints whether they play 'Erotic City' or not. The surprise is that a few who initially thought 'Erotic City' was far too graphic to program have been airing the song unedited and received less listener resistance than expected."

In his article, Walt spoke to Tolliver to see how our listeners were receiving the song. "Without breaking the law," Tolliver said, "my obligation is to play what the people want to hear. When an artist is as important as Prince, you can't avoid playing most things that he puts out because people want to hear it. Even when groups say some of the music is in poor taste, you really don't have much choice if you want to keep your station on top."

Initially, Tolliver switched from an uncensored version of "Erotic City" to an edited version in response to complaints from several community groups. The altered version of the song, he says, got "four to five times the number of complaints" that the original song drew. "People would call me and tell me, 'You're not playing the real version of that song. We want to hear the real version.'"

Rubie McCullough was the Executive Director of the Harvard Community Services Center. Ms. McCullough's battle with us over song lyrics started the year before when she objected to us playing another Prince record "Irresistible Bitch." McCullough, whose center ran a tutoring service, day camp, and other community services in the black community, says "Erotic City" was brought to her attention by concerned parents. As a result, the Harvard Community Services Center was one of the groups that initially pressured us about airing "Erotic City." "We worked with councilmen and seniors in the neighborhood. We had one sponsor (exert pressure on the station); there were even teenagers that were opposed to the song. That was the coalition we had," McCullough, told *Radio & Records*. "If they're playing it again, then we'll pressure WZAK again. We want that song off. Edited or unedited, we found it not conducive to good listening."

In Walt's article McCullough disputed Tolliver's claim that pulling "Erotic City" would be commercially untenable for WZAK. She even dragged Curtis Shaw, the GM of crosstown WJMO, into the controversy by claiming he said he "wouldn't put those records on his station for anything in the world, and WJMO's not out of business."

When asked by Walt if she holds songs like "Erotic City" directly responsible for moral decay she replied, "It doesn't help. We could be utilizing the time we use to play dirty records to teach some of our people to read and write so they can get jobs."

Tolliver responded by saying "When I was being raised my parents taught me you were not to repeat something if it was deemed bad. You'll eventually come across something that will have an effect on you, but if you've been raised properly, you'll be able to deal with it. Radio and TV have obligations to entertain, not to babysit or teach. Those jobs are for schools, teachers, and parents, who, to me, have fallen short of their responsibilities."

McCullough went on to complain that songs with controversial lyrics seem to be confined to black/urban radio. Tolliver responded, "Rock groups have been into drug lyrics, devil worship, and all sorts of stuff for years. These civic groups keep getting on our case, but say nothing about what happens on CHR and AOR stations." At that time WMMS was playing the song as well. "These groups need to quit listening to so much black radio and hear what the rest of the world is doing," Tolliver added.

Ultimately the controversy over playing "Erotic City" helped our visibility in the community and increased the "noise level" we always tried to maintain.

In 1985, Jeffrey Charles launched his "For Lovers Only" show, which became very popular. He played three hours of romantic music every night, and four on the weekends. Lynn had created the show in 1982, with the title coming from General Caine's album *Girls*, which included a song by that name. That song would open the show when Lynn hosted it, and when Jeffrey took the spot over; he wanted to get rid of it. "I hated General Caine's song at first," he said, "But Tolliver convinced me to try it a little longer. People started responding to it."

Listeners would mail in requests for the show; the station would receive more than a hundred letters per week on average, plus another fifteen or so phone requests each night. It was a throwback at the time to have a dedication show—a radio fixture from the 1960s. But people loved it. The most requested songs were "Always and Forever" by Heatwave, "Knock Knock" by the Dazz Band, and Luther Vandross' "A House Is Not A Home." George Benson's "Midnight Love Affair" was played every midnight. There was even a "For Lovers Only" club, which sponsored picnics, Christmas parties, and Valentine's Day events. It was the number-one-rated show in Cleveland in the 10:00 p.m.–1:00 a.m.-time slot in the Arbitron ratings.

In 1986, Lynn received a nomination for On-Air Personality of the Year by the *Billboard* Radio Awards, and in 1987, he received a nomination for the *Billboard* Radio Awards for Program Director of the Year. He had become a national figure earning the name "America's Bad Boy" for his involvement in controversial promotions. He was more mischievous but that doesn't have the same ring as bad boy. Lynn would say provocative things on the air and played some "naughty" records and he also "broke the rules" when it came time to some on-air giveaways. And we did our best to play up those "controversial" moments to burnish his "bad boy" image. Lynn was also named one of the top ten program directors in the nation by the industry magazine Inside Radio. They wrote that he "turned aside all urban challengers and managed to move the demos up while keeping the station hip and very close to the streets of Cleveland." He won the *Billboard* Radio Award for On-Air Personality and Program Director in 1990, 1991, and 1992. Bobby Rush, who was our music director at the time, was named *Billboard*'s Music Director of the Year those same three years. In 1990, we were the number one urban contemporary radio station, according to Arbitron. We had an 8.8 percent share of all Cleveland listeners in the Arbitron ratings.

Between 1981 and 1987 we tripled our share of our audience. By 1987 we were the number one station in Cuyahoga County, and third among listeners in the Cleveland metropolitan area, which included Cuyahoga, Medina, Geauga, Lake, and Lorain counties.

Billboard
RADIO
Awards
90

WZAK 93FM has been nominated by BILLBOARD Magazine as Radio Station of the Year.*

In addition, WZAK personalities have been nominated for these major awards...
▼ Lynn Tolliver, Jr.—Program Director of the Year*
▼ Lynn Tolliver, Jr.—Radio Air Personality of the Year*
▼ Bobby Rush—Music Director of the Year*

93FM
WZAK

1729 Superior Avenue, Suite 401, Cleveland, Ohio 44114. 216.621.9300
Represented Nationally by Durpetti & Associates

*Black Format, Medium Market

"That's a turnabout akin to transforming the Cleveland Indians into champions," wrote Bob Dyer of the *Akron Beacon-Journal* in 1987. The Tribe was 62-100 in 1987.

That year, WDMT, our main competitor up until then, switched formats to contemporary hit radio. "There's no pot of gold at the end of the rainbow because of the tremendous prejudice that exists with advertisers toward black radio," WDMT's general manager explained of the shift. With WDMT out of the market, we were the number one station in Cleveland and the only urban contemporary station in the metro. It turns out he was dead wrong. There was a pot of gold and we were going to get it!

Up until that point we never worried about how we ranked against the general market radio stations such as WMMS. It was around this time that we contemplated what it would take to become the number one radio station in the Cleveland metro.

In 1990, Lynn launched "Pillow Talk," which ran before "For Lovers Only" and was hosted by Bobby Rush. The show began with Bobby airing calls from listeners, who often requested Anita Baker, Natalie Cole and the O'Jays. Hearing the listeners make their requests on air was a major feature, and draw of the show.

We had famous recording artists coming in and out of the station all the time. LL Cool J stopped by when our offices were on Superior Avenue. Cleveland Central Catholic High School was across the street from our studios, and LL showed up for his interview around the time that school was letting out. Of course, the kids got wind of who was coming by, so when he left the station, there was a huge crowd of girls out front waiting for him.

It was always interesting to me that the artists who took the time to visit the station had long careers—those who had seen the ups and downs of the industry—were the nicest. The cockiest were the ones that had some huge initial success and were thinking it was always going to be that way. And it never is. An example of the former was Gladys Knight. She always came by when she was in town and she couldn't have been nicer. She was pleasant to everyone she came into contact with, from the receptionist to all the DJs and other staff.

By 1991, Cleveland became a majority-minority city. Our listeners were, of course, primarily black, but twenty to thirty percent were white. In a 1991 article looking back on the station's success for *Cleveland Scene*, Mike Hilber hazarded that WZAK was partially responsible for the declining power of WMMS, because "WZAK became such an influence in the market from a revenue standpoint. When you have a no-growth marketplace regarding revenue, the money has to come from somewhere. And even though I'm no direct competition with the general market radio station, I still feed out of the same trough. So the money that WZAK generated, which was in many cases general market funds, came out of somebody's pocket. When that happens, a radio station starts collapsing from within when you do not start meeting projections. They start changing their game plan. They cut back on promotion; they cut back on other things that increase their ratings. So it was like we were dropped from space into a no-growth marketplace, and that affected the market. It's leveled off now, but in the beginning, it shuffled the deck."

We were the only radio station in Cleveland, except for the classical station WCLV, to keep the same format for more than ten years. WMMS had changed their format to CHR, contemporary hit radio, in 1984. We had the same key staff in place—Mike Hilber in sales and Lynn Tolliver in programming. Our DJs included Kim Johnson, Kym Sellers, Lankford Stevens, Bobby Rush, Fred Williams, and David Tolliver. We had thirty-five people total on staff.

At our tenth anniversary party in 1991, we celebrated our success in style. We welcomed 8,500 people to a massive party at the Cleveland Public Auditorium, billed as "the biggest free party ever thrown by a radio station in Cleveland broadcast history." The line-up included the Wooten Brothers, LaRue, the O'Jays, Levert and the Rude Boyz, Riff, Keith Washington, Phil Perry, Kiara, and others. We gave away tickets on the air and had a thirty-two-person security force run by the Black Shield, the black patrolman's association. There had been rumors that gang members were planning to come and perhaps cause trouble, but that never materialized.

By then "Just the Two of Us" was one of our most popular shows. It aired every Saturday from 8:00 a.m. to 2:00 p.m. and originally featured Tolliver and Ken Allen. After Ken left the station, Ralph Poole joined Tolliver as co-host. Ralph was one of my favorite people I've worked with. He had an interesting path to local radio stardom. Ralph's sister Lynne was a friend of a local record rep named Pam Jones. Ralph tagged along to the station one day with Lynne, and it seems like he never left. He always had a positive attitude and volunteered to work at any event or do anything asked of him. He was always ready for more, and his engaging personality and infectious laugh endeared him to everyone he met.

"Hey, Ralph can you help clean out the prize closet?" I would ask him.

"Sure, no problem," would be his response.

"Can you take the van and have it washed?"

"Sure, no problem."

Tolliver started putting Ralph on the air to get him to laugh. He eventually started doing some board work and a bit of on-air work. I recall that when Ralph first started doing on-air work Ralph would be so nervous that the palms of his hands would become incredibly sweaty. It was as if he had just washed his hands and forgot to dry them. Ralph was a natural, and when he joined "Just the Two of Us" the show took off and became a habit for the urban community of Northeast Ohio. Oh, and did I mention that Ralph also was the promotion director for the station for a time until he became too important to the on-air staff?

Tolliver and Ralph would ad lib a lot of their Saturday show, which included riffing between the two of them, giving advice to listeners, and taking dedications and giving away a lot of prizes. We had such a demand from sponsors to give away their products that we developed an "instrument" to give them away without cluttering up the airwaves. We called it the Zak Pak. By offering us product to give away, our advertisers were trying to increase their exposure on our airwaves. The Zak Pak included everything we had to give away that weekend. It might consist of tickets to a movie premiere, coupons to a local restaurant, a new CD, etc. And usually to win the prize callers had to recite what was in the Zak Pak before they could win it. That gave our advertisers more recognition for their product.

By the mid-90s urban music was changing. Rap and hip-hop were becoming more popular and influential. In 1995 we introduced a show called "Phat Friday," hosted by Lynn's nephew Dave Tolliver and Antonio "Banana" Marshall, a part-time DJ and a full-time electrical inspector for the Illuminating Company. The show ran from 8:00 p.m.–1:00 a.m. on Fridays, and its tagline was "From da hood, for da hood." It included hip-hop, old-school soul, reggae, and rap. They also had characters, like a "gold digging home girl" called "Boo-Shika" and a lot of on-air joshing between David and Banana. They also talked a lot about current affairs, including racism. As one review of the show called it, "It's radio as raw and uncomplicated as a fresh bucket of chicken." Phatty Banks, a Cleveland rapper said of the show, "Banana and Dave are as real as you can get. And nobody else on the radio does the creative stuff they can do."

In 1996, there was another significant controversy over the music we were playing, similar to that of the late eighties, but this time it was national. A group called the National Music Review Council (NMRC) lobbied for federal regulation to oversee song lyrics. We already had the community advisory board from our city council run-ins a decade earlier. So we quickly formed a new committee when this flared up.

Kenneth Zakee, chairman of the 21st Congressional District Caucus's crime and safety committee, was incensed by the lyrics in "The Candy Rapper" by Bird and MacDonald. He wrote to the station with his complaint, and two of us went to the next caucus meeting and agreed to start a panel. The issue was getting a lot of national attention, and rather than let it get to the point of government intervention, we decided it would be good to do some self-policing. We were the first station in the country to establish a lyrics review board.

When the issue first garnered national attention, *USA Today* praised WZAK for taking proactive measures. "While the station reserves final rights on programming decisions, it has established a committee of Cleveland residents to pass judgment on the content of songs with 'questionable lyric content,'" the article stated. The panel included students, a district congressman, the city's director of student activities for the public schools, and a member of Cleveland's Teen Father Program. We tried to play edited versions of the songs by bleeping out what may have been "dirty" words. But our listeners complained because the wanted to hear the original, un-edited versions. We aired announcements urging parents to take an interest in the songs their children were listening to, as well as the television shows and movies they watched. We also would bleep out lyrics of songs that had no questionable content just to get people's attention!

I never felt the issue had much merit. I've never heard people say, "My child heard a gospel record, and now he wants to go to church." To me, it comes down to a stable home environment. You can listen to anything if you're brought up well.

WZAK was also a trendsetting station that had an enormous impact on music both locally and nationally. Cleveland brags about being the rock and roll capital, but I think that's somewhat questionable. The Rock and Roll Hall of Fame is here because every Cleveland radio and TV station got on the bandwagon and lobbied for it. *USA Today* reported that we crushed every other city in the country regarding city support during the nationwide vote. Personally, I think the Rock and Roll Hall of Fame should be in Memphis, but I'm glad it's here in Cleveland. I wish they had built in on Public Square and not on the lakefront, but that was Cleveland back in those days. Whenever there was a significant decision to be made, you could count on the city leaders to make the wrong one.

Although there have been a few memorable rock and roll singers to come out of Cleveland, there have been numerous nationally recognized R&B singers, such as Bobby Womack, The O'Jays, Gerald Levert, Bone Thugs-n-Harmony, The Rude Boys, Men at Large, and the Dazz Band. Akron has also spawned R&B stars, such as James Ingram and Howard Hewitt. We sponsored many of their concerts; the Dazz Band played at our first-anniversary party in 1982.

WZAK broke a lot of records and brought attention to a lot of new recording artists. Lynn Tolliver was responsible for that. As Sean Ross, who was R&B editor at the trade publication *Radio & Records* in the early 1980s, put it: "There are always two types of radio station program directors—those who want to play the hits and those who want to make the hits. The former group wants to avoid mistakes. The latter are the people listening to every new album looking for the next hit." Lynn Tolliver was definitely in that latter group. Sean used to listen to WZAK when he was a college student in Detroit, as early as 1981, because Lynn and WZAK were playing songs no one on Detroit R&B radio were playing. And Detroit wasn't slow on music, just different. As he puts it, "If the atmospheric conditions were right, you could hear WZAK in Detroit (although not clearly, you had to want to listen to them)."

Tolliver had his pulse on the community as far as musical taste. He always found songs that were not typical of songs that you'd expect to be on an urban radio station. He had broad musical taste because he had worked in Top 40 for a while, and he knew what people liked, black and white.

WZAK could make an artist's career. Lynn Tolliver often promoted new artists and helped them get their start if he believed in them. Tolliver is credited with breaking "Sara Smile" for Hall & Oates when he was programming WJMO. He launched the careers of Gerald Levert of the vocal group LeVert and the trio Next. He played Usher before anyone else, as well as Mary J. Blige's second record "Real Love." He was the first person to play MC Hammer on the radio. The R&B quartet Jodeci once took a private jet to make sure they got to one of WZAK's parties because the station was so instrumental in their stardom. Kevin Harewood was the general manager and COO of Hush Productions in the 1980s when the company was one of if not the most prominent music management companies in R&B, producing Whitney Houston and others. "Tolliver was so good at picking hits," Harewood recalls. "He was the first to play a lot of artists, including Freddy Jackson, Melissa Morgan. Some of the songs WZAK played first went on to become number one singles. Tolliver just picked records that weren't on to yet." Lynn also promoted Cleveland artists. He was from Cleveland and he had a lot of pride in the talent that was here, so he wanted to support local musicians.

Lynn was the program director, and at first he also did the afternoon drive shift from 3:00–7:00 p.m. As our most popular on-air personality, it made sense for him to work morning drive, and he eventually moved to that time slot. Kim Johnson, the Kym Sellers, and Ralph Poole joined him over the years. It was a grueling schedule because he was on the air six days a week and still had his programming duties. In hindsight, it was too much to ask of Tolliver. To make it easier for him, we installed a remote studio in his home so he could do the show from there. That worked for a while, but it was still a heavy workload.

In 1997, we made what most people thought was an incredibly risky programming change: replace Tolliver and his crew on the morning show with the syndicated "Tom Joyner Show." I felt confident that we were making the right decision and fought hard to make it happen. Tom Joyner had become a legendary DJ because of his daily commute between Dallas and Chicago. He hosted an urban morning show on KDKA in Dallas then would hop on a jet and fly to Chicago and do the afternoon drive at WGCI. His nickname became the "Fly Jock." When he first announced this gig, I thought it would last a few weeks, perhaps months, and then he'd either drop dead from exhaustion or say it was all a big stunt. Well, months later he was still at it, and the show was getting more popular in every market. ABC Radio Networks was syndicating "The Tom Joyner Show," and they put a lot of resources into the program. So while we had a hard time getting Cleveland Mayor Mike White to be on our morning show, Joyner had President Clinton on as a guest.

I feared that a competitor could decide to switch formats to urban or urban adult contemporary (a format focused on black adults ages twenty-five to fifty-four), put Joyner on the air and then we'd be in a real battle. A switch like that would

Tom Joyner on the move!

UP! UP! UP!

Demo	Winter 97	Summer 97	% Increase
Persons 12+	6.5	8.0	+23%
Adults 18+	5.9	7.3	+24%
Adults 18-34	11.5	13.5	+15%
Adults 25-54	6.5	8.8	+35%

*Source Arbitron Summer 1997

Tom Joyner
weekdays 6 am - 10 am
The Media Store
2510 St. Clair Avenue • Cleveland, Ohio 44114
216/621-9757 • Fax: 216/771-4164
Represented nationally by D&R Radio

93FM
WZAK

THE MEDIA STORE

have been very easy for a competitor to do. I thought it was critical to stop that before it happened. We negotiated a good deal with ABC, and on the morning of January 5, 1997, we debuted "The Tom Joyner Show". Tom was well received by our audience. There were definitely some growing pains. We tried to include a lot of local content during his show but that didn't always sound great. We were interrupting the flow of the Joyner show. Eventually we figured it out and never looked back. The best part of it all was we still had Tolliver and his talents. I was thrilled with how it turned out in spite of the seemingly risky move. Joyner is currently still on the air around the country, but as I write this book, Tom Joyner has a firm date for retiring. He's a real pro who has worked his tail off to be successful. And he's a super nice guy.

WZAK became famous in Cleveland because Lynn built a solid structure. As he puts it, "I'd always been about building the fort. If you create a fort, and you fortify the fort, the fort will protect you. That was my foundation. A lot of the jocks that I was around earlier, they didn't understand that; it was always about their ego, their personality, and their career, not the station." Lynn noticed when he promoted the station more, even if he didn't promote himself, listeners remembered him. Building up the station was his dominant role, not being a disc jockey. One time, when he worked at the AM station WJMO, he was in the car with a friend and Rick James's "Super Freak" came on. His friend asked, "Is that JMO?" Lynn told him it wasn't. "Turn to JMO," his friend said. And Lynn thought: "Right in the middle of Rick James? Wow." That meant that the station meant more to listeners than the song. It fortified Lynn's theory that DJs should always promote the radio station first.

Lynn says WZAK is the best radio experience he ever had. At WZAK, he was allowed to be a part of all the elements of the station, not just the on-air product, but also the other factors that went into making WZAK what it was. Lynn was involved in the sales process as well as the on-air and off-air promotions. For the jocks it was never simply playing records and tossing out the time and the weather. As Lynn remembers, at other stations, even as a program director, "You may not have had any say. You may not have had any input. At other stations, the DJ's, they're often at each other's throats on the same stage. I didn't understand that. I'm thinking, 'Hey, this DJ comes on in the morning, and that DJ comes on in the afternoon. Why are they at each other's throats?' They are on the same team."

Lynn's approach to programming was unique. He was always innovative, and most of the record companies did not like him because he would listen to the album and try to pick the song that he thought was the best song for his audience. He saw that there were some artists that everybody liked—somebody like Aretha Franklin. He would never choose another artist over Aretha or The Temptations—even in the nineties he gave The Temptations their last hit. And later with rap, groups like the Sugar Hill Gang. Lynn used to stress how to know if we were playing the right record, with all the records that are available. If the next record coming up was "Truly Yours" by The Spinners, how did he know that it shouldn't have been Aretha Franklin's "Spanish Harlem"? Tolliver didn't, but if he played as many great records as possible, it was hard to lose. He also had a theory for why an individual likes a particular song. For the most part, he believed, women are into words and a softer texture, and men are into elements like rhythm and are not really into lyrics. When you have all those elements in place—the words, the music—it's difficult to beat.

Tolliver's philosophy was to let the DJs be free and not to nitpick their style, as some program directors did. He wanted to earn their trust and give them freedom.

"Phat Friday," the show that his nephew Dave Tolliver and Anthony "Banana" Marshall did together, was the show Lynn hated the most. I think he disliked it so much because of a generational thing. But it was one of the hottest shows so he let them do their thing.

Lynn designed a system called "freedom within a structure," and a color code along with it: red for the hottest records, blue for medium, yellow for new, and green for not-so-hot. The hottest records had to be played often to fit with people's listening habits. Very few people would listen for three hours. They might get in their car and listen for only a half an hour, but they would listen to the station every day. If the hits didn't come up in that half hour, the listeners were disappointed. Most successful radio stations spend a lot of time and money on researching what songs to play and, more importantly, what songs to quit playing and when. We called 125 listeners each and every week to determine what songs our audience had tired of. And it wasn't just some random 125 people. We needed people who were in our target demo of urban radio listeners between the ages of eighteen to forty-four. So to get 125 people to participate in this research we had to call 500 people each week! It was a huge expense but paid huge dividends. You'll find that no matter what listeners say about repetition and tight playlists, they want to hear the hottest records and the hottest music. The music that the audience wants to hear is not always what's the newest; it could be a song that's been out for seven months, it could be a song that's been out for a year. You have to be able to play what they want to hear.

Lynn believed that WZAK was the only station that played all requests legitimately. Growing up listening to the radio, Lynn used to think, "Man, those jocks, damn, they are fast." A guy might call in, and the DJ would say, "And what would you like to hear?" The caller would say he wanted to hear "Help" by The Beatles, and then right away the song played. When he started to work in radio, he realized that all those calls were pre-recorded. That felt dishonest to him. At WZAK, when we played a request, Lynn told the DJs, "Hey, if you answer the phone and the guy asks for 'Let's Get It On' by Marvin Gaye, let's say that you play it. And then two calls later, somebody asks for that record again, play it again." He wanted his DJs to take requests seriously.

Some of the times, Lynn could tell whether or not a record would be hot. For example, when the group Next sampled Kurtis Blow's "Christmas Rappin'" as the basis for their song "Too Close," automatically it was comfortable, and the single got huge. He could even tell when records that he hated were going to be big. The Gladys Knight and the Pips single "I've Got to Use My Imagination" definitely wasn't for him, but it hit number four on the *Billboard* Hot 100. He was only truly wrong about one record: "Disco Queen" by Hot Chocolate. He didn't think that was going to make it, but it did.

By 1992, there were discussions of easing FCC ownership laws, allowing for more consolidation of the industry. At the time a broadcaster could own up to twelve AM and twelve FM stations nationally and one station of each frequency in a given market; the changes would permit a broadcaster to own up to thirty AM and thirty FM stations nationwide, and double its station holdings in a given market. I could see the writing on the wall. In the spring of 1992, I predicted that it would be a "eat or be eaten" environment if the rules changed. We started getting calls long before the rules changed from radio brokers fishing to see if we had an interest in selling. Deregulation changed the landscape of radio. There was a bubble developing in radio then. Wall Street money started pouring into the radio industry, and as station values rose, we started wondering how we were going to expand the business. We were trying to buy other stations using our own money and bank debt. The bank would loan you maybe five times the station's cash flow, but by the mid-1990s stations were being sold for ten-to-fifteen-times cash flow. So we had to make up that difference (50-67%) with our own money or other people's money, or we would not be able to acquire new stations.

We kept growing and succeeding. Bobby Rush continued to be popular with his "For Lovers Only" show that aired Sunday through Friday evenings from 8:00 p.m. to 1:00 a.m. We were the first in this market to do a love songs show. Arbitron ranked Rush first in the 7:00 p.m.–midnight time period among persons over twelve and those twenty-five to fifty-four with better than a 12 share in each segment. He was also first among eighteen to thirty-four year-olds with more than an 18 share.

Our best year ever was in 1992 despite a downturn in the economy. Our success was due to keeping true to our format and we did not try to make big plays to add white listeners. Tolliver observed that sometimes when urban contemporary radio stations think that they have peaked with their black audience they try to increase white listenership by changing the product. We never did that.

Another key to our success is that our programming department, including our DJs, were always involved with the sales and marketing side of the business—they understood the whole radio business, not just the music part.

The following year saw even more success: we swept the nominations for the *Billboard* Radio Awards, including Best Station, Best Programming/Operations Director, Best Music Director, Best Promotions/Marketing Director, and Best On-Air Personality. In 1994 we refocused our energies on our music programs to attract the 18-to-34 demographic, increased our promotions, and rose even further in the Arbitron ratings. We did a promotion with Outkast and Geauga Lake Amusement Park. We gave away $930 in gas in a "Free Gasoline" promotion, which led to long lines outside gas stations. We worked with Louis Stokes's 21st congressional district on community service projects, and we sponsored the 93FM Children's Choir.

In 1996, we topped the Arbitron ratings as the number one station in Cleveland—not just in the black market, but overall! We were the most-listened-to station in Cleveland for listeners aged twelve and up. It took us fifteen years, but we finally did it. It was a turning point for the station and for the market overall. Other markets had urban stations that had reached the number one position but this was new to the Cleveland market. I think it made a lot of people uncomfortable but the new reality was something that we had anticipated for a long time. That year I also succeeded my father as president of the station, as well as the four other stations we owned at the time. My father became Chairman of the Board. I promoted Lynn to VP/Director of Operations. I was fortunate to have a father who gave me so many opportunities and also encouraged me to expand the business and take on new challenges.

In 1998, near the end of our ownership of WZAK, the National Association of Broadcasters nominated us for a Marconi Award for Major Market Station Urban of the Year. The nomination read, "WZAK-FM recently celebrated seventeen years of urban contemporary programming. A combination of solid leadership and dedication to the community it serves makes WZAK a worthy nominee for Urban Station of the Year. Recently WZAK adopted a Cleveland elementary school. The station's staff would tutor students and participate in school programs. WZAK also held the Million Penny March, which raised more than $15,000 for Cleveland charities. According to the latest Arbitron, WZAK is the number one radio station in the Cleveland metro. WZAK also has one of the highest sales power ratios among all radio stations."

That year our programming efforts were at their zenith. The fall 1997 Arbitron results that came out in January 1998 showed us moving from number two with an 8.7 share 12+ to number one with a 9.9 share. We were also ranked number 1 in the eighteen to thirty-four and eighteen to forty-nine demos. In the big money demo of twenty-five to fifty-four, we ranked number two with a 10 share, virtually tied with Oldies WMJI, which had a 10.1.

We were always fortunate to get a lot of coverage and support from the trade magazines, especially from Walt Love at *Radio & Records*. In March 1998, Walt inteviewed Bobby Rush and Lankford Stephens for a detailed story about our rise to the top. Bobby Rush became the programming director of WZAK in June 1995 when Tolliver was promoted to operations manager, and the first thing he did was promote Lankford "The Man" Stephens to assistant program director and music director. Bobby had been a DJ and the music director at the station for a total of twelve years. He was a native of Cleveland, so he knew the city and its people.

In the interview, Bobby explained to Walt that our primary target was the twenty-five to fifty-four demo and our secondary objective was the eighteen to thirty-four demo. "Quite frankly we want 'em all, but we have our targets to keep us focused," Bobby said. Walt mentioned that the station reminded him of the mainstream R&B stations of the seventies and eighties from the standpoint of being able to satisfy the black community and the general populace who want to hear black music presented with "flavor." Bobby responded by saying, "We've always had to sell ourselves to a broader audience beyond the African American community." Bobby added, "The fact that WZAK doesn't have any direct urban competition at the present time means we have to do a variety of things that are all positive. When you have direct competitors, you sometimes have to take the narrow approach and just buckle down on one target. But, in our case, we've been able to do things a little differently."

MARCONI RADIO AWARDS

MARCONI RADIO AWARDS

MARCONI *Radio* AWARDS

FOR EXCELLENCE IN

Chantilly Ballroom, Loews Anatole Hotel, Dallas, TX — Saturd

$\mathcal{N}$ominees

R

MO-AM, Seattle, WA
T-AM, Cedar Rapids, IA
TC-AM, Minneapolis, MN

ge Market Personality
he Year

Johnson, WDIA-AM, Memphis, TN
Kevoian & Tom Griswold,
FBQ-FM, Indianapolis, IN
e Murphy, KCMO-AM, Kansas City, MO
ne Perkey, WHAS-AM, Louisville, KY
n Tolliver, Jr., WZAK-FM, Cleveland, OH

Classical

KING-FM, Seattle, WA
KKHI-AM/FM,
  San Francisco, CA
KLEF-FM, Anchorage, AK
WCRB-FM, Boston, MA
WQXR-FM, New York, NY

Black/Urban

KKBT-FM, Los Angeles, CA
WHRK-FM, Memphis, TN
WRKS-FM, New York, NY
WXYV-FM, Baltimore, MD
WZAK-FM, Cleveland, OH

As Bobby mentioned, we had no direct urban competitor at the time but I was always paranoid that we would get a competitor. Doing urban radio isn't easy. In fact it was pretty damn hard. We had virtually every asset in our arsenal to beat back any potential competitor, but we never let our guard down.

In the article, Bobby expounded on his programming philosophy by saying, "Each demographic has grabbed onto the different varieties of programming we offer, and they've embraced us and what we do throughout the week. We've studied and continue to explore the likes and dislikes of people in Cleveland."

Walt thought it was obvious that in the city of Cleveland, mainstream Urban Contemporary radio not only continues to live on, but it also wins, and wins big! Other urban contemporary stations that cover the demos with huge numbers like this are few and far between, Walt added. "What we do by putting all of these different shows together creates a nice flow that's unique. We flow from Joyner to Tolliver, to Kim Johnson, to Lankford, and then, on Saturdays, to the WZAK Mix Party. These are all specialty shows unto themselves, but they all have a proven following, as you can see by our ratings all week and in every daypart. Each of our shows is like a runner handing off the baton to the next person to do better. By the time we get to the end of the day or the week, we got 'em," Bobby replied.

On the subject of mainstream urban contemporary stations not being able to be all things to all people as they once were, Bobby said, "We all have to remember that each market is unique unto itself and each audience is different. Our job is to know our listeners and then try and please them at all times."

Bobby and Lankford were the decision makers when it came to picking our music at that time. Lankford "The

Man" Stephens had been the program director at WDAO/ Dayton where he was very knowledgeable about what music was resonating with our listeners. And like all of our air personalities, he was always out in the community. Music selection is key to any radio station, but because of our broad demographic appeal, it was especially tricky for us. The key to our success was a consistent formal and informal audience research.

When Bobby and Lankford were asked by Walt on how we pick our music Bobby said thought it was about all the air personalities being here in this market for many years. "We are all constantly out in the community and in the club scene, where we get a feel. We use a combination of formal research, local research, and our local knowledge of our listeners." Lankford added. "We have gotten to know what people respond to over a period of time. We also take into consideration national charts like those in *Radio & Records*. We look at what's happening on a national level. Then we have local retail sales information that we also take into consideration. Plus, we have our local call out research on what's hot and what's not in the market. All of this information helps us come up with the correct music mix for our audience in our market." Lankford continued.

At this point in the development of WZAK one of the major factors in our success was that our air staff worked well together and we didn't have a lot of turnover. "I really think listeners feel comfortable after a period of time knowing that an air personality they enjoy is going to be there every day just for them," Lankford said. "We become like special friends to them because, over time, we get a one-on-one relationship going, and that's what we want. That's when the listener begins to count on us. They look forward to hearing us each day, and God knows we look forward to them being there every day for us playing contests, making requests and asking questions about the station and/or the artist we play. So I think longevity and consistency are not only a plus, they are a must."

Programming was the first pillar when it came to building WZAK, but without the other two—sales and promotions—we would have been a one-dimensional station and not built to last. We needed the other two so that we would have a solid foundation to grow.

THE SALES PILLAR

When WZAK first switched formats in 1981, the person we hired to be our general sales manager was a guy who was living in Denver. He had been recommended to us by Gordon Stenback, the general manager of WZZP. One of the things that appealed to us about this candidate was that he had worked in Cleveland radio in the past so he was able to tap into his network and got some appointments to pitch the station to local media buyers and advertisers. He was more of a rah-rah kind of manager and not a strong leader who could put together a strategic sales plan, much less execute that plan.

He didn't last long. His wife wanted to stay in Denver, so he was commuting every week to Cleveland. One Monday morning he didn't come into the office. We were concerned that something may have happened to him. This was before the days of mobile phones so communicating was a bit more difficult. Later that day we received a FedEx envelope with his letter of resignation and the keys to a car that we had secured for him. He left the car at the airport with instructions on where to find it. That would be the first time we would experience the flakiness of people who thought of themselves as professionals. I don't know if that was unique to the radio business, but it was a good lesson. In hindsight it was a positive for us in that it forced us to look for a new sales manager, and essentially his departure led us to hiring Mike Hilber.

Mike had been unhappy at WGCL, the Top 40 station in Cleveland. Mike said that after fighting all day long to bring in a sales order at WGCL he'd have to fight the internal staff to get the order on the air! That was a valuable lesson for us. We did whatever it took to reduce that internal friction so that the ads would run and we could generate revenue.

My dad got in touch with Mike and invited him and his wife Irene to join my parents for dinner. When the waitress came by to take their drink orders, Mike's wife Irene declined, since she thought she might be pregnant. It was the first time they had met each other, but my mother looked at her and said: "Oh, are you pregnant?" Irene was still unsure, but my mother knew. Their first child Michael was born seven months later.

Mike hesitated when my father offered him the job. He was unsure he wanted to work at a black station. At that time, moving from a general market radio station to an urban/black radio station wasn't considered a smart career move. But he was so enamored with my parents that he eventually accepted. It was a difficult transition for him. On his way to the office for his first day of work a guy covered with tinfoil was taking a leak in a bus shelter right outside our front door. "Welcome to ZAK," he thought.

In his first week on the job Mike asked us, "Do you guys have a network?" And we said, "No, what's a network?" A radio networks supplies programming elements to radio stations across the country. In exchange for being able to use those programming elements the radio station airs commercials from the network. In the media biz it's called barter. A few weeks later Mike signed a network affiliation network that generated $300,000 in ad revenue for the station. That was huge money for us at the time, more than we had generated the entire first year of WZAK as an urban radio station. At that time, Cleveland was a much bigger radio market than it is today with annual revenues of in 1982 of $26.7 million. Mike knew Cleveland was an important market for any radio network, no matter how bad or low ranking the station might be, if you had the Cleveland market in your network, it was a feather in your cap. There was a pot of money you could get from national networks then, and it included ABC, CBS, NBC, and all the other networks that fed radio programming to local radio stations. After a few years we didn't use many of the programming elements but we still aired the commercials because we wanted—and sometimes needed—the revenue it generated.

My father allowed Mike a lot of freedom to run the department as he saw fit. Mike would pop into my office and say, "Hey Lee, I've got an idea, what do you think?" Sometimes he would sell sponsorships to programs that did not exist yet. Once he came back to the office after an appointment and said, "Hey, Lee, I just sold a battle of the bands."

I looked at him, confused, and asked, "What battle of the bands?"

"The one I just sold," he said. So then the programming department had to go and create a battle of the bands weekend feature! That's how we operated in the early days. Bringing in revenue was paramount.

Mike was a hard-driving manager and recruited staff that responded to his management approach. Some thrived and others did not. I likened it to how different sports coaches had different styles. You had Bobby Knight on one end of the spectrum and Tom Landry on the other end. Each was successful but did it with very different approaches. Mike held a department meeting every Monday morning and individual meetings every Wednesday. He would meet with each salesperson and plan their week with them. He expected them to follow the plan they agreed on. It was not a good meeting the following week if they didn't have a good reason for not following the plan.

We had some superstar sales reps on the team. Renee Singleton (who made the transition from promotions director), George Cohn, Bill Cook, Sharon Williams and Baron Brown are just a few of the people on the sales team that were instrumental in our success. My sister Maria had been focusing on sales before Mike started, and at first it was a challenging transition for her to report to him. But she was incredibly successful, partially because she worked so hard to not seem like "the boss's daughter." She felt she had to prove that she was not getting special treatment, and she also felt a responsibility to show the family in the best light. It was not easy. She was young, and when she had her first child, she was back at her desk three months later.

It could be hard to convince many clients to consider advertising on WZAK because they were apprehensive, based on their ignorance of what the black community represented. And although our ratings were decent in those early days, buying ads on our station was not a no-brainer for some advertisers. It was a constant struggle to get people to advertise because urban radio had never been sold from a qualitative standpoint. Before we came along, many of the other urban radio operators at the time were satisfied to get their advertising budgets from black-targeted products: ethnic hair care products, malt liquor, and that kind of stuff. What we wanted to do was bring the power of the black community to a broader set of advertisers, and stress to those advertisers how vital the community was to their marketing efforts.

One of the other chall-enges of working in urban/ black radio back then was what you might call "hidden racism." It was pretty subtle, but after a while you could pick up on it pretty quickly. I remember one guy at an ad agency asked us, "How many black business owners do you have listening to your station?"

Mike replied, "Do you ask Magic 105.7 (the oldies station) how many white business owners listen to their station?

No? I didn't think so."

I'm sure it still goes on today, but hopefully it is not as prevalent. This may sound odd, but when I worked in urban radio in Atlanta the racism was much more out in the open, which was easier to deal with from a business standpoint. You're not interested in the black consumer? Great, there are many more businesses that are so thank you for not wasting my time. In Cleveland it was not as blatant, so many times we wasted our time trying to get to a "yes" from someone who was never going to advertise on our station.

Of course, there were also a lot of misunderstandings and ignorance about the black community. For instance, when explaining why they did not want to market to the black community, people would often say things like, "there's like an 20 percent unemployment rate in the black community" (According to Wikipedia in 1982 and 1983, the black unemployment rate skyrocketed to above 20 percent for a nine-month period starting in October 1982 which was about double the national unemployment rate.). We would respond, "Well, what about that 80 percent that are working?" That was always a "light bulb moment" for those advertisers.

One of Mike's strengths was his ability to take a lot of information and distill it into something that could be communicated effectively and easily. He developed a five-point presentation of why advertising on WZAK made sense. These were the five points:

Population: The black population of Northeast Ohio was large. In the metro area it was almost 20 percent, and in the city of Cleveland it was 50 percent.

City within a city: There were more blacks living in our listening area than all people living in Wheeling, West Virginia. This helped people visualize how big the black consumer market was in Northeast Ohio.

Time spent listening: Black listeners listened to WZAK

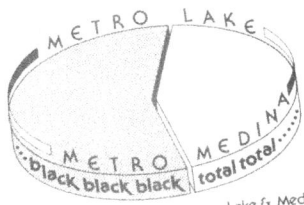

for longer periods of time than listeners to most other radio stations in town with the exception of WCLV, the classical station. Part of it was our compelling programming. The other part was that there were fewer choices on the radio dial for black listeners.

Qualitative: Blacks consumed certain product categories at higher rates than the general market. We focused on a lot of those categories.

Location: We could identify many zip codes where blacks were the majority of the population. We focused our sales efforts on retailers, restaurants and other businesses in those high-density black areas.

A lot of people didn't even think about reaching the black community, and even if they did, they didn't think of it in those terms. They thought maybe their general advertising would reach them, but more often than not it wouldn't.

We got early support from the LaRose family's House of LaRose, the distributor of Budweiser. They were very supportive, and great people, but they were not doing it to be nice. They did it because it was good business. The Cleveland Coca-Cola bottling company was another large early account, as well as McDonald's, both nationally and locally.

One of the strengths of our sales team was our ability to generate national sales dollars. National sales came through our national sales rep who represented WZAK along with other stations across the country. Their job was to pitch WZAK to national advertisers like K-Mart. George Cohn was our longest serving national sales manager and he did a tremendous job generating revenue from national accounts. About a quarter of our sales revenue came from national accounts.

We had a very diverse group of advertisers, which was a huge advantage. None of our advertisers represented more than a few percentage points of our total sales. By not being beholden to one or two major advertisers, we were never in a position to have to compromise our programming or promotions to satisfy an advertiser.

We reached out to every possible company to advertise on WZAK. We had an advantage in that we were popular in areas of the metro that other stations did not have an influence in. Mike would walk into the offices of big customers—say, the May Company—who had a number of locations, and put a star on a map that was the high-density black area map that they served. And he showed them the map and would say, "I bet that's your worst store. I bet those are your slowest sales." They never said, "Oh, yeah, you're right," but he could see by their reaction he was correct. So then he would say, "I bet you're chalking that up to the neighborhood. It's not the neighborhood; it's your marketing." Then he would explain: "You think your marketing is spot on because you

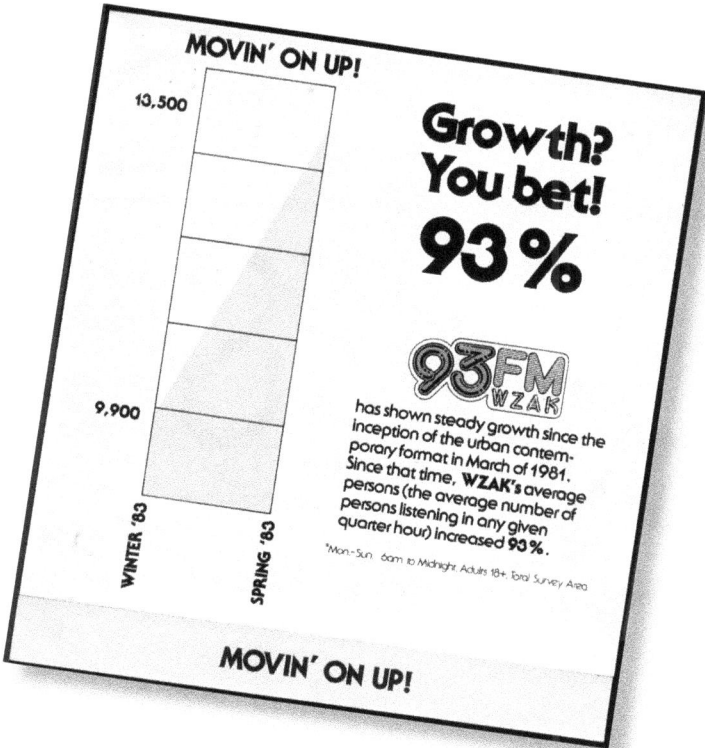

MOVIN' ON UP!

13,500

9,900

WINTER '83

SPRING '83

Growth?
You bet!
93%

93FM
WZAK

has shown steady growth since the inception of the urban contemporary format in March of 1981. Since that time, **WZAK's** average persons (the average number of persons listening in any given quarter hour) increased **93%**.

*Mon.-Sun. 6am to Midnight, Adults 18+, Total Survey Area

MOVIN' ON UP!

are airing a TV commercial on *Murphy Brown*. Well, I've got to tell you, in the black neighborhood; *Murphy Brown* is not a big deal. All I want you to do is take just a small portion of your marketing budget and devote it to the store in the black community with the slowest sales." He would convince them to do this by advertising for the store on WZAK. It worked every time. It worked because we did have a high concentration of people who lived near that store, and they did listen to WZAK. And they responded to advertising just like everybody else does.

Sometimes advertisers were reluctant to advertise because they thought they could only advertise niche products to black consumers. If Mike and one of our reps went to the advertising account representative of a grocery chain—places like Giant Eagle or Kroger's, they might say, "But what would I advertise to your listeners?" We would respond: "How about bread, milk, and meat? The black community buys staples too!"

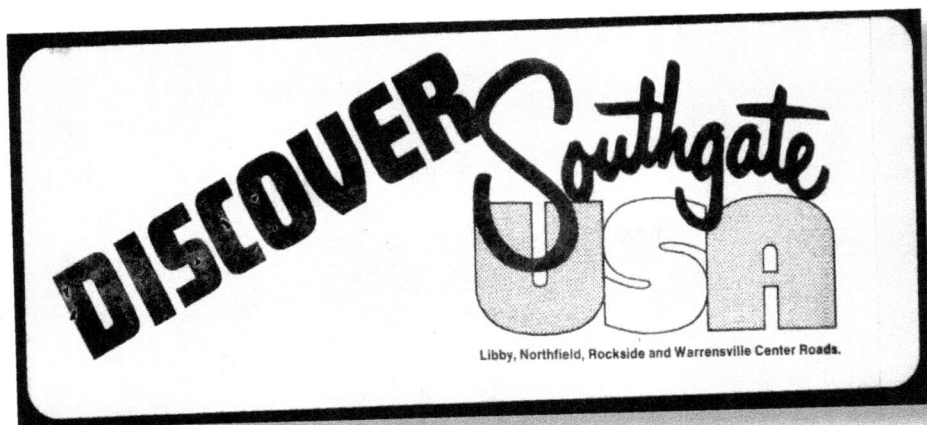

DISCOVER Southgate USA

Libby, Northfield, Rockside and Warrensville Center Roads.

Because advertisers didn't know much about our consumer segment, they had no idea how to communicate to the black audience. On many occasions the black consumer just wanted to be invited to shop somewhere and to be recognized for their value. And black shoppers know when they're being invited. So if we picked up those two or three stores they had in a high-density black area, those people at the company who bought the ads become heroes because sales would increase. Advertising on WZAK worked.

We also had what we called a "Need Meter." That meant that the more an advertiser needed to reach the black consumer the more aggressive we were on our pricing. During elections, we were able to generate a lot of revenue from politicians and ballot issues wanting to reach the black voter. We focused a lot of attention on this business during the election cycles. Other categories of advertisers that rated high on our "need meter" were black hair care companies, concerts that targeted the black audience, soft drinks and a number of others.

Our past experience as an ethnic radio station made us realizes that the black community is no different than any other ethnic community. They have different tastes, they have different ways of expressing themselves, but everyone wants the same thing. They want to be successful; they want to spend time with their families, travel, etc. In a sense, when we changed formats we went from trying to appeal to multiple ethnic groups to appealing to one large, more homogenous ethnic group. Not that the black community is homogenous, but they're identifiable, and one of the great things about having a black audience is that when you ask them to go somewhere on behalf of an advertiser, the advertiser sees it. "Oh, I see more black people in my store!" If you advertised on any adult contemporary station, whether it was Magic or WDOK or WQAL, and white people are in your store, you don't know if they are there because of a radio ad or a TV ad. So that was a significant advantage for us.

We spent a lot of time and effort marketing to advertisers by sending them a lot of promotional material. Mike wanted each sales promotion piece to be brief and impactful. He would demonstrate how much time we had to make an impact with our pieces by opening an envelope and in the same motion taking the paper out of the envelope and putting into the trash. Our pieces focused on the value of the black consumer, the number of black consumers and how important the black consumer is to businesses operating in northeast Ohio. We were infamous for going direct to clients and bypassing agencies. We also utilized our station events and concert co-sponsorships to entertain our clients. We wanted our reps to have personal relationships with all of their clients. Good relationships helped when, on the rare occasion, our ratings fell short.

And we've already established that some clients never advertised with us because of racism. So we just went around them. Mike would go higher up. The higher up you move in the chain of command, the less racist people are because those executives just want to make money. So, as we put it, we never took "no" from the person who couldn't say "yes." We just kept moving up the ladder until we found someone who would appreciate what we were talking about from a revenue standpoint.

A lot of times this approach got us in trouble. Many of the ad agencies did not like us because we went around them and directly to the client, and then the client would come back to the ad agency and tell them they wanted to advertise with us. That would make the agency look bad. And on top of that, when we knew the decision to buy from us was coming from the client, we'd charge very high rates. That's how we became the top biller.

For many years, one of the disadvantages of owning a black radio station was that black radio couldn't convert their audience share into an equal share of advertising revenue. For example, if you have a ten share and the market is a 100 million dollar advertising market, you should generate 10 million dollars worth of advertising by converting your share into advertising dollars. That's what's called a power ratio. News/talk stations and other more general market stations traditionally had higher power ratios. To us a high power ratio was the target. It would indicate that we were punching above our weight class.

Black radio's power ratio was like a 0.6. So you had a ten share in audience and you're in a 100 million market, but you're only generating six million dollars instead of ten. In my opinion, it was

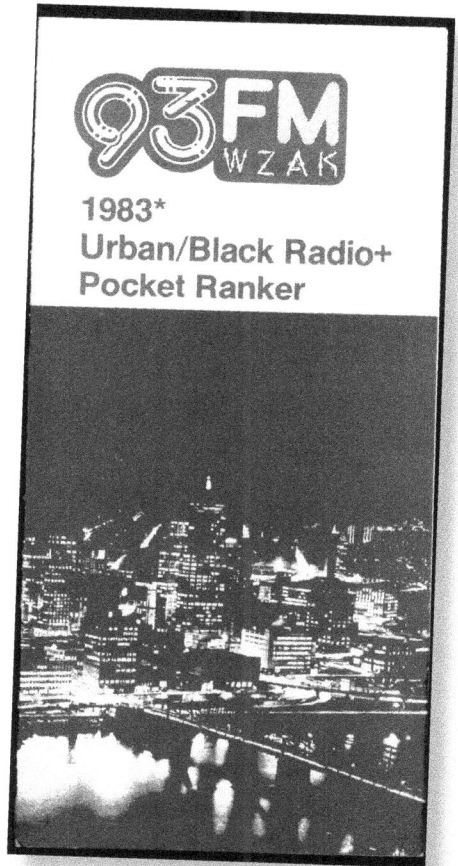

93FM
WZAK

1983*
Urban/Black Radio+
Pocket Ranker

that black radio wasn't aggressive enough on the ad sales part of the business. They were satisfied with their share of dollars targeting the black consumer but didn't go after the general market dollars with the same gusto that we did. I think that some black stations did not receive the same level of attention from owners, and far more marketing dollars were spent on general market stations because the owners just did not know how to advertise to their audience. I'm sure there was some bias at play, but I think it was a minimal effect.

Of all our accomplishments, one of the ones that I was most proud of is the fact that we had achieved the highest power ratio of any urban radio station in the country, which was a 1.6. We would routinely achieve a 1.6 power ratio. Advertising sales came not only because of our hard-working sales team, but also as a direct result of our high-quality programming. Without our promotional team, though, we wouldn't have had a leg to stand on.

93FM WZAK

1988 WZAK LISTENER CALENDAR

THE PROMOTIONAL PILLAR

I have always enjoyed working in promotion/marketing and special events. I grew up hearing my dad tell stories of the events that he and my mom produced to promote their Greek radio program. Event marketing was just coming into its own back then. Today it is a multi-billion dollar industry and virtually every media brand uses events to connect with their audience and advertisers.

After graduating from Cleveland State University and working at WZAK for a few months, I decided to look for another opportunity. I was hired to be the communications coordinator for the development department of the local office of the American Heart Association. Development is a fancy word for fundraising. Our department did a number of things, but primarily we produced events to help raise money and awareness. I learned more in one year from my boss Dennis Zack and our events coordinator Rick Karikas than I did in all the years of schooling. Dennis and Rick knew how to create exciting and compelling events, how to promote them, and how to generate revenue. When I left the

AHA a year later to work full-time at WZAK, my goal was to do the same thing with the station when the time was right.

I believe that our promotional efforts were equal to our sales and programming efforts, and they undoubtedly created a stir around Cleveland. Our goal with our promotions and live events was to increase the "noise level" for the radio station and to keep us "top-of-mind" with our listeners. "Top-of-mind" translated into higher Arbitron ratings.

I knew it was important to establish a strong identity for the radio station. MTV had launched in 1981 and I always loved their logo and how strong it was. I knew we had to have something similar. I hired my friend Bransilav Ugrinov to create our new logo. (Branislav had developed the distinctive "Z" logo for WZAK when we tried the easy listening format.) He came up with a strong 93FM logo in bright colors. Eventually he added the WZAK to the logo and made a couple of more slight modifications over the years but the logo that WZAK is using today is the same one we started with almost 40 years ago.

The earliest effort to establish WZAK as *the* station to listen to was when we utilized "guerilla marketing" at the Earth, Wind and Fire concert at the Richfield Coliseum on November 10, 1981. Wikipedia defines "guerilla marketing" as a marketing/advertising strategy to promote a product/service with little or no money. That was the operative word in the early days of WZAK...little or no money. WDMT was the presenting radio station for the concert so we had to be a bit more creative to get our message out to the listening public. I arranged to have our DJs do a video welcoming everyone to the show. We produced it at the Coliseum's video studios and then played it on their big video screens a bunch of times before the show started. In addition we passed out promotional flyers to every car as they paid for their parking. Our team then spread out inside the Coliseum and distributed a souvenir pass that looked like a backstage pass to the show. We were everywhere we could be with the message that WZAK was on the rise.

Station-produced events became the cornerstone of our promotional efforts. We had to create our own events because when we changed formats to urban contemporary we were the new kids on the block. Most Cleveland events already had relationships with existing radio stations, so we could wait around and beg to be part of a local concert or event or we could create exclusive events that we could control and reap all of the benefits. Events became so vital to us that we eventually formed a separate company called Big Bang Event Marketing to produce events for ourselves and for other local businesses.

As we approached the first anniversary of our format change, we decided to throw a party to celebrate our success. Our first major event, which became our signature event and the bedrock of the station, was the WZAK Anniversary Party. The first one was held in the Grand Ballroom of Stouffer's Inn on the Square in downtown Cleveland and featured Cleveland's own Dazz Band, which at the time had a massive hit record "Let It Whip." Tickets were free, but the only way to get a ticket was to win one by being the ninth caller when we played "Let It Whip." Using that on-air giveaway technique, we were trying to increase the time people spent listening to the station, which in turn increased our audience share. Almost 2,000 listeners attended. Needless to say there were glitches in the production of the event such as names not being on the guest list, but none of the attendees noticed. Our audience had a great time and it signaled that WZAK was a force to be reckoned with. Station concerts were rare at that time, but my father and mother had been organizing similar events since the 1950s. We were just putting our own urban contemporary spin on it. The success of that first anniversary party inspired us to look for other opportunities to create signature events.

IN CELEBRATION
of the
8th Anniversary
of the
GREEK RADIO PROGRAM
4-5 p.m. Sundays—WDOK
Xenophon & Lula Zapis

PRESENT THIS

DANCE & STAGE SHOW

HOTEL CLEVELAND BALLROOM
Sunday, September 30, 1956

In January 1983, two years after we had become an urban contemporary radio station, President Ronald Reagan signed the Martin Luther King, Jr. holiday into law. In the first few years we celebrated the MLK holiday with some special programming on the actual day, but eventually we turned the entire month of January into a celebration of Dr. King's life. We had short and long form programming features and our DJs appeared at local celebrations. And of course, all of those on-air and off-air features had sponsors attached to them.

February was a very active month for us because it was Black History Month. We took every opportunity to generate sales and positive PR for the station. We organized events around the city to recognize Black History Month. We worked with the Regional Transit Authority (RTA) and arranged for black history bus tours of Cleveland hosted by our DJs. Those tours sold out every year. We also worked to make Black History Month relevant to our listeners by featuring prominent local African-American leaders on air and at events.

We became a calendar-driven promotions machine. January was MLK Month, February was Black History Month, and after the success of our first-anniversary party, March became our anniversary month. June was designated as Black Music Month. As we moved into the summer, we didn't need to produce our own events to get our name out because there were so many local events that we were involved with.

Even though summer was a busy time for us we were always looking for ways to increase engagement with our listeners. Memorial Day is traditionally the start of the summer driving season. Each Friday of Memorial Day weekend we found a local downtown gas station to give away free gas to the first 93 drivers who got in line after hearing our announcement. I always looked for a gas station that was close to the local TV stations to make it easy for their news crews to cover the giveaway. It was guaranteed to garner local news coverage because the TV news broadcasts always attached it to a story about how the price of gas was compared to last year "but not for these people at the Shell gas station at 30th and Carnegie."

As we would head into the fall we looked at creating another "tent pole" event. I came up with the idea for the WZAK Turkey Jam. The inspiration for the Turkey Jam came from a big polka dance that Tony Petkovsek, the producer of the Slovenian radio show on the old ethnic WZAK, hosted every year. Every Thanksgiving evening, after people had their Thanksgiving dinner, they'd head over to a Slovenian community center and continue their partying, dancing the polka into the early hours of the morning. As Tolliver said, there's nothing new under the sun, just new combinations. So I took the idea of the polka party and married it with an urban listener appreciation party and called it the Turkey Jam.

The first year we had the Turkey Jam was in 1983. It was held on Thanksgiving evening and followed the same script as our anniversary party. Tickets were free, and the only way to get them was to win them by being the ninth caller when we played a sound effect of a turkey gobbling. The key to the anniversary parties and our Turkey Jams was creating the perception that tickets were hard to come by and if you got one you had scored big time. Our first Turkey Jam was packed, and everyone had a great time. We had a national recording artist as the highlight of the show and a DJ to spin music for dancing before and after the performance. And with a lot of sponsors attached to the event, it was a win for our listeners, our advertisers, and, naturally, the station.

To keep the Anniversary Party and Turkey Jam fresh every year, we had to continually reinvent them without departing

COTTON CLUB
CIRCUIT CITY
Where Service is State of the Art
93FM WZAK
Budweiser
THE 12TH ANNUAL
Turkey
JAM
FRIDAY, NOVEMBER 25, 1994
at the CLEVELAND
PUBLIC HALL AUDITORIUM
featuring
USHER, TONY TERRY
HOWARD HEWETT and MORE!

from their essence as listener appreciation parties. We did this by changing the venue, bringing in the latest hit recording artists, incorporating more sponsors, and finding new ways to give away tickets. We continued to give tickets away on the air, but we started creating sponsorship packages so that listeners could now go to local retailers and get tickets by purchasing something from those local stores. That move helped us generate more revenue and created more excitement because more people could participate in the event. And it made the tickets we were giving away on the air more valuable because there were fewer opportunities to win by calling in to the station.

Most of our events or promotional ideas for WZAK would start with me thinking "wouldn't it be cool if..." Wouldn't it be cool if we could send someone to see the opening night of Prince's *Purple Rain* tour? Wouldn't it be cool if we could send a listener to Los Angeles for the premiere of *Beverly Hills Cop*? That's how our promotions would go. I would tell my dad, Lynn, and Mike what trends I saw emerging, or what events or happenings I wanted to capitalize on. And we would move on it, creating a promotion to tie into the trend. We were right on top of everything.

At a station Mike had worked at previously, they had a signature song that when they played it, it would trigger a contest. Be the ninth caller and win something, etc. We all agreed that a signature song would be a great thing to have.

We were trying to come up with a song so recognizable from the first notes people would know what song it was. We settled on Kool & The Gang's

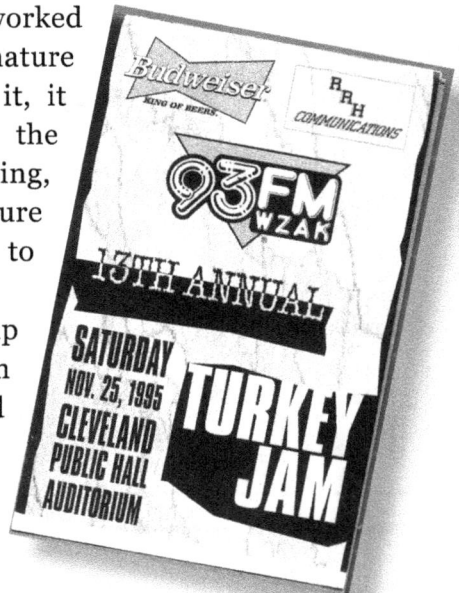

Budweiser
KING OF BEERS

R R H
COMMUNICATIONS

93FM
WZAK

13TH ANNUAL

SATURDAY
NOV. 25, 1995
CLEVELAND
PUBLIC HALL
AUDITORIUM

TURKEY JAM

"Celebration." The opening has that funky, upbeat intro and the "woo, woo" that signals fun. There was something so infectious about that song that it permeated the attitude of our on-air sound. "Celebration" became our signature song for virtually every contest we did going forward.

To build on the brand of our signature song, we created the Celebration Card. The Celebration Card was the size of a credit card size that we would distribute at personal appearances and shows. We'd encourage people to register their card by sending back the postcard that was attached to the card with their name, address, and birthdate. We created a database long before most other stations had listener databases. At one point we had over 40,000 names, and we could break them down by zip code, age, birth date, etc. We created our own version of Valpak using our database of Celebration Card holders. We'd mail people coupons from our sponsors (which, of course, they paid for to be included), and we'd tie those into our on-air promotions.

Cash giveaways were a big part of our promotional efforts. We tried being strategic when we gave away our cash. Thursdays were the first day of the Arbitron diary, so we would try to give away more money on Thursdays with the thought that we could influence diary keeping the rest of the week. The goal of the cash giveaways and every on-air contest was always to get more people to tune in to the station and for those already listening to listen longer. Those are the only two ways to increase your ratings.

93 FM
WZAK
celebration card
215633

93 FM
WZAK
celebration card

REGISTRATION FORM

Name_____

Address_____

City_____

State_____Zip_____

Telephone No_____

Age_____ MALE ☐ or FEMALE ☐

Where did you pick up card?

_____

Signature_____

IMPORTANT! You must fill out and return this registration form with your Celebration Number to qualify for prizes.

Celebration Card No._____

We always tried to keep the cash giveaways fresh by changing things up. Sometimes we would add bonus dollars, or change the winning number caller from nine to ninety-three, or something like that. Other times we would give a bonus to the cash winner who also had a registered WZAK Celebration Card.

One of the things we did that caused a lot of excitement and word-of-mouth was when Lynn Tolliver would play "Celebration" ten times in a row—with a new winner every time. He'd say that he had locked himself in the studio and that he was in control of the station now. The phones would light up, and we would pretend we were pounding on the door, trying to get Tolliver to stop playing the song and trying to get someone to unplug the transmitter. Then the next day we would say Tolliver was suspended for flaunting the rules. Most people knew it was all a ruse—they got that it was a stunt—but they loved the fun of it. The reactions of the winners were phenomenal, and of course, we would record those and play them over and over again throughout the week. That also gave the illusion that we were giving away more money than we were!

One of the things that we learned from doing market research was that more substantial cash prizes did not significantly encourage more people to participate. In surveys, we would ask our listeners if they would tune it for the chance to win $10,000. About 94 percent said that they would. When we asked them if they would tune it to have a chance to win $1,000, 92 percent said they would, and when asked if they would tune in to have a chance to win $93, 88 percent said they would! It was a valuable lesson and stretched out marketing dollars.

We were always pushing the envelope trying to come up with unique methods to connect with our listeners and to give our advertisers a way to reach our valuable audience. We purchased an interactive voice response system that we named the ZAK Line. It was essentially a large phone answering machine. Before the Internet, people would call an 800 number to find the time, weather, listen to clips of new songs, etc. We did those, but we also offered a zodiac forecast on the ZAK Line. We got thousands of calls a week on the zodiac line. The woman who did the forecasts did them for free because there was an option at the end of the call to set up an appointment with her for a private reading. And of course, we sold sponsorships to the ZAK Line. One of the more effective capabilities of the ZAK Line was it could also make outgoing calls. We loaded the Celebration Card database into it, and every evening the ZAK Line would call the phone numbers of people in our database with a pre-recorded message from our of our jocks inviting them to tune in at a specific time to hear "Celebration." By holding a registered Celebration Card, you had inside knowledge of when we were giving away money.

A lot of radio stations don't do promotions like that anymore. It was a different era when smaller, more nimble companies owned most radio stations. Today, most stations are owned by large corporations, and to get something like that approved they would have to go through so many layers of bureaucracy that they never try. Also, you could never get away with some of the stunts today because you'd have some intern posting something on Facebook or Twitter, letting people know it was a prank. But we had a lot of creative, innocent fun back then. And once we had sold all our advertising spots at the highest rates, we needed to push the envelope to bring in additional revenue.

Personal appearances were another key component to our success. Our jocks were extremely popular in Cleveland. They were often the most recognizable people in the black community. Lynn Tolliver was our most famous air personality; as an east sider, he used to have to go to movies on the west side because if he'd go on the east side, he'd be bombarded with listeners asking for prizes and photos. Cleveland was, and still is, a very segregated city, but, as Lynn Tolliver put it, "Cleveland is a one-on-one kind of city. You've got to be able to touch each listener. You've got to touch them by showing yourself, by being out there with them—no matter who it is. In the past, no one has done that for the black community here. All the others have only been on the radio—nothing personal. We took it to the streets."

We would do appearances at shopping areas, retail stores, nightclubs, concerts, and grand openings—everywhere you could imagine. We would park our promotional vehicles out front, and the people knew that the jocks were inside. They knew we would be giving out prizes and that there were good times to be had. Advertisers would always give the DJs a stipend for showing up, and we did a minimum of two personal appearances per week. I think some DJs may have earned more from personal appearances than their programs. The non-air staff also made themselves very visible by attending these promotions. We all went to all the parties. We all showed our faces everywhere. At those grand openings, we were there, dressed to the nines, our station button on our lapels.

We used to do a lot of free-with-purchase appearances, too. So, let's say that we had a handful of tickets to the circus, or Cedar Point, or an Indians game. We would package them for the retailer, who would tell people that if they would come in and buy a certain product, they would also receive free tickets. It was a smashing success. For example, Kentucky Fried Chicken would do a free-with-purchase deal. People would come in, buy the meal, get the tickets, and then leave without their food. They just wanted the tickets. They'd line up to get into these places. They would have to put up felt ropes to keep everybody in line.

Here's an example of how many and what types of promotions we were doing. In June 1989, this was our schedule:

- Rhodes High School tour of the station
- A parade and wheelchair race downtown
- Free pizza and aprons handed out on downtown's Mall C for one of the food festivals
- A club blitz bumper sticker giveaway (a club blitz was when our DJs would go out as a group to local clubs to pass out promotional material)
- A Cleveland public school "Ride a Bus with Us" promotion, where Jeffrey Charles and other DJs rode RTA busses all morning or afternoon
- The Heritage Days festival in the Flats
- Hosting the Miller Beer Sound Express
- Appearing at the opening night of the movie *Batman*
- Giving away free tickets to and having an event at the opening of the Spike Lee film *Do the Right Thing*
- A dance at the Ritz night club
- A picnic at Luke Easter Park
- Participation in the Cleveland 300 auto race parade

You get the idea. We tried to be everywhere every day.

In 1984, we were in a pitched battle with WDMT for urban supremacy. They had organized an autograph party with the group DeBarge on April 18. We were determined to stage our own event to steel their thunder. We decided to hold a breakdancing competition that we called the "Street Dance Monopoly." It was to be our biggest promotion by far, up to that time—and it caused a considerable stir. Break-dancing had become an international phenomenon, so we invited kids to come to the Stouffer's Inn on the Square, where the Renaissance Hotel is now, for a dance competition. We worked with the hotel management and its security. The hotel requested that we hire additional security because there were so many calls inquiring about the break dancing contest. We complied with their wishes by supplying eight uniformed off-duty police officers. And we hired another seven people we had worked with before from the Fatherhood, a local fraternal organization, that works as ticket takers and helps with crowds at large arena events.

They were going to audition, and if they got into the competition, they were going to perform and be judged later that evening. But we made the mistake of hosting it on a Friday afternoon, not realizing that school was out that day because of the spring vacation. It was general admission—the first 2,000 people to arrive would be admitted. But about 6,000 people showed up! Kids started lining up outside the hotel—some dressed like Michael Jackson—as early as 10:00 a.m., even though the event was not going to start until 6:00 p.m. Part of the reason for the overflow crowd: the youngsters were invited on a first-come, first-served basis. In retrospect, issuing tickets would have definitely been the way to go. They started dancing while waiting in line. Public Square became impossible to navigate. They had to close it to traffic and reroute all the buses. The local news media started flooding the place, too—TV cameras came out, and they were broadcasting live from Public Square.

Police and our DJs got on bullhorns and asked the crowd to disperse, but they didn't want to leave. Before the doors were to open at 6:00 p.m., the crowds trying to get in broke some windows. Around 4:00 p.m. it was determined the crowd was just too big to handle, and we decided to cancel the event. Tolliver left his air shift, came down to the hotel, and stood on top of a police car with a bullhorn, announcing the event was being cancelled. He also told the crowd the event would be rescheduled and to listen to the radio for further details.

We had done these kinds of promotions before, but we had no idea that the turnout would be so large. We had always catered to an older audience, and we weren't prepared for the enthusiasm of the younger members of our audience. We pioneered most of the promotions in the Black community like this. When we planned the contest we knew these events were popular in cities like New York. What we didn't realize was how popular it was going to be in Cleveland! Since we already had some promotions on the air, we didn't want to make things more cluttered so we decided there wasn't enough airtime to give away tickets on the air.

We dodged a bullet so to speak because there were no injuries or fatalities. Asked by a reporter to comment on the chaos I said, "we underestimated the popularity of the event"—the understatement of the year!

But it was also a learning experience. Despite having to cancel it, there were no injuries, incidents, or arrests. People were excited to be part of the event. And promoters contacted us afterward about co-sponsoring events because we proved we could generate a crowd. We made national news: *USA Today* covered it, among others. We held the rescheduled competition, at the Front Row Theatre, a few weeks later. It attracted a crowd of 3200. This time we asked listeners to write in for free admission tickets to the event, and they did. We had enough requests to fill the house three or four more times. We probably could have sent out 10-12,000 tickets if we had put it on in a larger place. That time, the event went off without a hitch and was a huge success.

The aborted 'Street Dance Monopoly' put us on the map among all residents of Northeast Ohio. Our listening audience responded positively to the event and the rescheduled event became a defining moment in the ascension of WZAK. And it completed drowned out the autograph party that WDMT had organized with DeBarge. Mission accomplished. But if I had to do it over again I would have approached it much differently. It was a high risk, high reward event and we got lucky.

We did a lot of controversial promotions and billboards—some were award winning. The idea behind trying to generate controversy was to extend our impact because we did not have a lot of money to spend on advertising. We were trying to create greater awareness by word of mouth, by doing something outrageous, and it worked. People talked about us, the media picked up on it, and politicians protested. And we kept doing them because the formula worked.

One of our most controversial contests played off the LL Cool J record "Big Ole Butt" that came out in the summer of 1989. We worked with a popular club downtown to award a prize to whoever had the biggest butt. It was a pretty innocent promotion that was based on a song that was getting a lot of national attention and airplay. The usual suspects came out and complained about the promotion and got the local news to pick up on their manufactured story. The contest went off without a hitch. *The Plain Dealer* gave us "Jeers" for the contest in their "Cheers and Jeers" section. They wrote: "Perhaps it makes no difference to radio stations and their on-air personalities that they come off as crass, tasteless, insensitive, juvenile, ugly, sexist or racist in such silly plays and displays for listeners, or perhaps they truly know their audience and feel it is easily amused. Or perhaps insulting the listener and playing to the lowest common denominator is the only goal of such a sorry excuse for a promotional gimmick." I'm not sure why but that contest and the resulting controversy followed us for many years.

In the latter years of our ownership, we produced an event that focused on the power of black women called "Sistas." It was held at the CSU Convocation Center (now the Wolstein Center) and featured vendors who were marketing to black women, nationally recognized entertainers, major celebrity appearances, fashion and hair shows and prize giveaways. It was a colossal success. My only regret was that we didn't start producing it years earlier.

The limited TV advertising we did was just to give us some spice and to get people talking about us. The foundation of our advertising efforts was always outdoor advertising. This included billboards and transit ads. Billboards are my favorite form of advertising. You have seven seconds to get your point across, and when they are done right, they are a thing of beauty. One of the advantages of targeting the black community back in those days was that the majority of the black audience in Greater Cleveland resided in a handful of zip codes, which made them easier to target with billboards. We had a lot of different designs over the years, and we would blanket the market with our boards. One of the tricks I learned back then was to have new locations every month for our boards. It would cost more in paper because you had to print more billboards, but it paid off in the long run because each month when they posted your new boards some of the old ones would stay up because they hadn't resold them to any other client. So we got bonus coverage for very little extra cost.

During a visit Los Angeles, I saw a billboard for radio station, I think it was KLOS, posted upside down. It didn't cost any more money, but it always got you more attention. We'd get phone calls all the time from listeners letting us know that one of our billboards was upside down. I think the technique still works but you hardly ever seen anyone use it.

Transit advertising was another great tool for us. KISS-FM/WRKS in New York City used this to great effect, and I nicked it from them. We focused on the bus lines that covered the east side, where most of the black community resided. I wanted every bus traveling between the east side and downtown to have our sign on the front of the bus. It was a great tool and always increased our visibility, and it was the cheapest sign to buy on the bus. Back then RTA had busses that would just make a loop downtown helping commuters get around town, and in those days a lot of the ad agencies had their offices downtown. I advertised heavily on the loop bus line to so that downtown agency workers and business owners saw our ads, which made it seem as though we were everywhere—even though the loop busses were cheaper to advertise on than the regular east and west side lines.

Our billboard advertising also earned us criticism from certain circles. We did a billboard that featured our morning team of Lynn Tolliver, Ralph Poole, and Kym Sellers. Tolliver and Ralph were naked but held signs in front of them to hide their "private parts" with Kym in the middle looking befuddled. We also did one featuring a black woman holding a microphone and laying on top of Tolliver, with the caption "Getting You Up and Getting You Off in the Morning." We received a fair amount of backlash for that one. We did another billboard campaign to promote our promise to play ten back-to-back hits in a row—without interruption. In the ad, we showed ten women in bathing suits standing side-by-side, shot from behind. We chose white models so people couldn't say we were exploiting black women. That got a lot of attention and brought out the naysayers again. Were these ads self-consciously provocative? Sure, but obscene? That seemed like a stretch.

LES

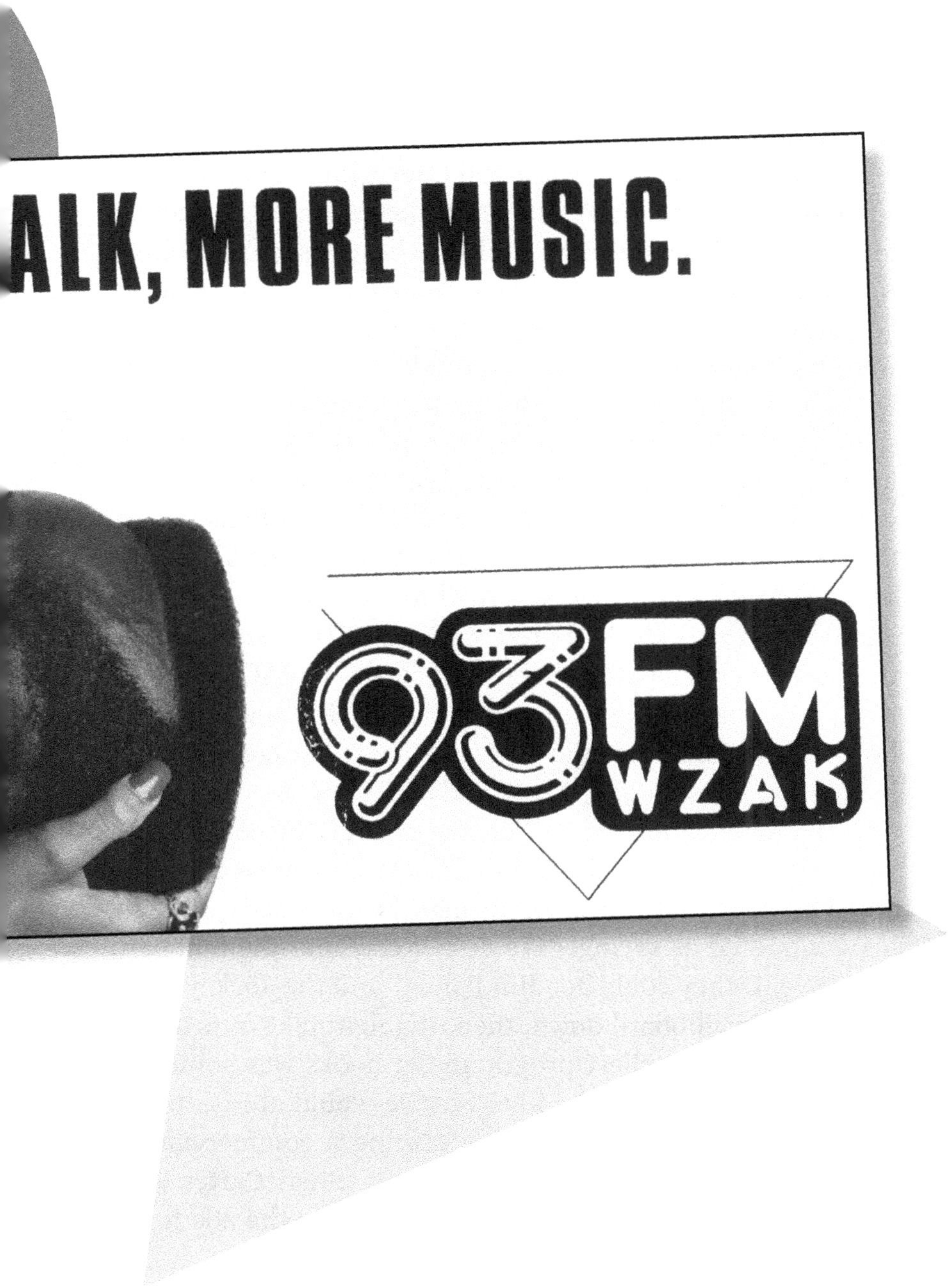
ALK, MORE MUSIC.
93FM
WZAK

One of our less risqué ads showed a woman holding a man's mouth closed with a scarf so he couldn't talk, with the tagline "Less Talk, More Music." We did a TV version of the billboard that showed a man moving his mouth real fast, and a woman wrapping something around his mouth to get him to stop talking to reinforce that we played more music and talked less than other stations. It seemed utterly innocuous to us, but some people said that it depicted violence. The RTA declined to use the ad on buses or trains. The Grassroots Political Action Committee of Cuyahoga County (G-PAC) found the ads sexist and racist. We started to think that perhaps we were insensitive, so we polled our listeners and asked if they felt they should be taken down. Listeners overwhelmingly said we should keep them up. We felt G-PAC was mainly looking to get themselves in some headlines. We were curious what sort of advertising they wouldn't find offensive, and they asked us to put up billboards that said "The Three Hits of Life: Reading, Writing, and Arithmetic." We refused. Then we went out and put large red "CENSORED" signs on top of the controversial parts of the billboards. G-PAC countered with a letter-writing campaign calling for an advertiser boycott. Cleveland Cavaliers president Art Savage responded by writing us saying, "We would urge you to discontinue advertising which may be offensive or could be construed as racist or sexist," but did not pull advertising per se. My father stood his ground: "This is our form of freedom of expression," he was quoted as saying. "We do not consider the billboards offensive. If they could get Jim Palmer and the Jockey shorts to take their billboard down, then we might take ours down."

One of our earliest programming hooks was something we called "Fourplay." The idea was we would always play at least four songs in a row before playing a commercial. We used TV and billboards to promote this. Sheri Carter was a model from Cleveland, and we cast her to do the ads for us.

She was terrific. She went on to host a local urban TV show called *Soul Soundtracks* that WZAK helped produce. She then moved on to BET and hosted a show with Donnie Simpson.

One particular stunt generated the most outrage of anything we ever did. In 1987, we held a promotion that would give twenty dollars to the first thirty people to show up at our studios at East 18th and Superior with underwear on their heads. It was just a silly prank that I heard on a rock radio station in Atlanta. Of course that radio station was a rock station so when they did the stunt, no one complained of any racial undertones. Our problem was we told people at 7:00 a.m. that we would give the cash away at 9:00 a.m. That gave people two hours to line up at our offices. Needless to say the crowd that showed up was larger than expected, we decided to offer twenty dollars to the first 100 people. The crowd continued to grow, hitting over 300 people. The police were called in, but there were no incidents or arrests.

The city council, however—notably councilman Jeff Johnson—considered the context racist and exploitative. Johnson sponsored an emergency resolution condemning our promotions and asking the mayor and director of parks, recreations, and properties to prohibit us from accessing public property. It passed unanimously. Johnson also lobbied to have our license revoked by the FCC: "My goal is to take the license away from Xen Zapis and give it to responsible people," Johnson said. He was also offended by an earlier promotion we did offering a prize to a person who brought in the largest cockroach, which he claimed demeaned the poor.

My father sent Johnson a letter that outlined the station's commitment to community service. We always had a robust community-giving component to the business. We raised money for the United Negro College Fund, the NAACP, and the American Cancer Society. In 1989, we won the Community Service Award from the National Association of

Broadcasters for our "Scholarships for Minority Students"; we awarded nineteen $1,000 scholarships that year. But it was the those promotions that what made the headlines. In his letter, my father mentioned that in the first few months of 1987 alone we had given to United Black Radio, made school appearances with the governor, conducted school tours of the neighborhood, and contributed to the WZAK/ Josephus Hicks scholarship. "Why don't you come forward to recognize these many worthwhile programs?" he asked Johnson. "I venture to guess it is because the news media would not give you coverage. And that is the same reason we choose to stage unconventional promotions: to get our name in the news. We will continue to stage unconventional promotions, and we will continue to lend our support to those organizations that are committed to improving the quality of life of our listeners. And I'm sure you will continue criticizing. That's life in Cleveland."

In the end, we did issue a public apology for the underwear campaign. We donated two $2,000 scholarships to the Cleveland Board of Education and agreed to form a community advisory group to review future promotions. "We apologize, and I apologize on behalf of my staff for some of the overzealousness that has been used in some of the promotions," my father wrote. "We don't want to embarrass the community or downgrade the community."

We continued our community service, of course: In 1988, just as the AIDS crisis was becoming public, Lynn Tolliver distributed thousands of safe sex kits around the city. Two years later, we received an award from the radio industry for a "community awareness project that was ahead of its time and subject to some criticism when it launched. Before everybody else got on the bandwagon, WZAK was putting the word on the street." Lynn told me that he felt WZAK was being scapegoated for problems in the black community. "There is a feeling that the black male and the positive black male role model has been eroded ... WZAK has only brought attention to that problem," he said.

For the most part, these controversies only helped us: we discovered that any type of publicity—as long as you haven't molested a child or killed somebody—works for you. We weathered those storms. After we grew more significant and more powerful, we continued to receive more pushback on our promotions and advertising campaigns. We worked hard to maintain good relationships with the black community despite that; the majority of our staff was black, many were with us for a long time, and they were all very involved in the community. That helped heal wounds.

One of our most successful and engaging endeavors was the Million Penny March. It was a takeoff on the name Million Man March. Ralph Poole led the Million Penny March, to benefit for Cleveland charities. He spent every day for a week walking through Cleveland neighborhoods collecting pennies in a wheelbarrow. At the end of the week, he had collected over 1,500,000 pennies, totaling more than $15,000!

I could write a hundred more pages about our promotional efforts but I think you get the idea. Advertising/marketing/promotions are the fuel that kept the engine running. And that's true for any business, not just for a radio stations. As Ted Turner liked to say, "Early to bed, early to rise, work like hell, and advertise."

Photographs in the Carol M. Highsmith Archive, Library of Congress, Prints and Photographs Division

THE LEGACY OF WZAK

In 1998, my father and I had lunch with Milt Maltz and his son David. Milt Maltz was a legendary broadcaster, and he told us that he had recently agreed to sell his TV stations to the media conglomerate Raycom. If Milt Maltz was selling, we thought it might be something for us to consider. I'll never forget what Mr. Maltz said to my dad over lunch: "Xen, if not now, when?" He also cautioned us never to "fall in love with something that can't love you back."

A few months later, we accepted a deal to sell our stations to Chancellor Media. They purchased six stations, (WZAK, WZJM, WJMO, WDOK, WRMR & WQAL) for a total of $275 million. When it closed in January of 1999, it was the most significant deal to date in Cleveland radio history. The new owners chucked the whole Celebration Card program at WZAK and changed the format of WZJM to Jammin' Oldies. Instead of taking audience share from Magic 105, they took audience share from WZAK, the cash cow. That's not how I would have managed the company, but they weren't our stations any longer.

Watching this unfold from afar taught me a valuable lesson: Just because somebody works for a big company, they're not any smarter than those at a small family businesses. In the old days working for a big company gave you access to a lot of resources. Not today. Everyone has to do more with less. It's much more of a challenge to try to come up with creative ideas on a small budget. Leonard Bernstein said it best: "To achieve greatness, you have to have a plan and limited time to do it." That's what we did with WZAK for those fabulous seventeen years.

I remember once saying to Lynn, Mike and others, "One day we will look back and think of this as the good old days." I was right. Those were magical years. We proved you could run an urban radio station and bring in major advertising dollars. My father—and I'd like to think me and my sisters also—created a fantastic culture that allowed us to have fun while doing great work. Steve Jobs once said, "It doesn't make sense to hire smart people and tell them what to do; we hire smart people so they can tell us what to do." That pretty much sums up my father's philosophy. He hired smart people, and they told us what to do. And fortunately, we listened.

When I think back on our successes and failures I can see a common thread from the original ethnic programming on WZAK to our ascent to the top of the Cleveland ratings. Excellent programming, robust sales, and effective promotions were the elements that made the Greek radio program that my parents produced a fixture with the local Greek-American community. Those three elements were also what made urban contemporary WZAK a ratings and sales powerhouse.

Like a three-legged stool, we created a stable foundation for the ongoing success of WZAK. I believe that that solid foundation is why, almost forty years later, WZAK is still at or near the top of the ratings in Cleveland.

Ultimately I like to think that we mattered to our staff, to the listeners and our advertisers. And we mattered to Cleveland.

ACKNOWLEDGMENTS

I want to acknowledge many of the people who were a part of the success of WZAK. Either by word or deed, the following individuals knowingly or unknowingly, helped in the development of WZAK: Gordon Alderson, Ken Allen, Bill Becker, Rich Bongorno, Baron Brown, Daryl Brown, Debbie Pirori Buckley, Ray Calabrese, Cyndi Cawthorne, Jeffrey Charles, Dwight Chillious, Kevin Chillious, Steve Church, George Cohn, Bill Cook, Tony Durpetti, Dale Edwards, Tom Embrescia, Eric Faison, Mitch Faulkner, Frank Foti, Avery Friedman, Joe Frolick, Barry Gabel, Joe Garner, Don George, Kevin Harewood, Mike Hilber, Jim Hooley, Lynn Huss, Rebbie Jackson, Sue Jansik Serra, Kim Johnson, Pam Jones, Al Kazlauckas, Jim LaRose, Tim LaRose, Krysten Livingston, Mike Love, Walt Love, Harry Lyles, Chris Maduri, Jacqui Majers Lachman, David Maltz, Milt Maltz, Mike Matonis, Chris Mavros, Barry Mayo, Bruce Mittman, Andre Morgan, Richard Nash, Mary O'Brien Mecke, Susan O'Connell, Thano Pasalis, Lynne Poole, Ralph Poole, Tina Rice, Eric Richards, Ruben Rodriguez, Sean Ross, Dean Rufus, Bobby Rush, Lynne Salivaras, Dale Santa Maria, Jane Scott, Kym Sellars, Renee Seybert, Brad Seybert , Lee Simonson, Renee Singleton, Kim Skillern, Willie Smith, David Sowd, Lankford Stephens, Roy Stipe, Marie Stover, Donna Thomas, Scott Thomas, Debbie Thompson, Lynn Tolliver, Barb Tranchito, Branislav Ugrinov, Mirjana Ugrinov, Al Warmus, Sharon Williams, Glenn Wright, Maria Wymer, and James Wymer.

My hope is that all of them look back at the time they spent in each other's orbit and remember it fondly.